北京外国语大学王佐良外国文学高等研究院出品
北京外国语大学“双一流”建设项目成果

外国文学研究文库 · 第五辑

The Idea of Culture

文化观念

［英］特里·伊格尔顿 著
Terry Eagleton
殷企平 导读

外语教学与研究出版社
FOREIGN LANGUAGE TEACHING AND RESEARCH PRESS
北京 BEIJING

WILEY

京权图字：01-2023-5354

图书在版编目（CIP）数据

文化观念 = The Idea of Culture ：英文 /（英）特里 · 伊格尔顿（Terry Eagleton）著 ；殷企平导读. -- 北京 ：外语教学与研究出版社，2024. 10. --（外国文学研究文库）. -- ISBN 978-7-5213-5662-5

I. G12

中国国家版本馆 CIP 数据核字第 2024P1Z033 号

出版人　王　芳
项目负责　邢印姝　徐　宁
责任编辑　徐　宁
责任校对　都楠楠
封面设计　奇文云海
出版发行　外语教学与研究出版社
社　　址　北京市西三环北路 19 号（100089）
网　　址　https://www.fltrp.com
印　　刷　三河市北燕印装有限公司
开　　本　650×980　1/16
印　　张　12
字　　数　237 千字
版　　次　2024 年 10 月第 1 版
印　　次　2024 年 10 月第 1 次印刷
书　　号　ISBN 978-7-5213-5662-5
定　　价　52.00 元

如有图书采购需求，图书内容或印刷装订等问题，侵权、盗版书籍等线索，请拨打以下电话或关注官方服务号：
客服电话：400 898 7008
官方服务号：微信搜索并关注公众号“外研社官方服务号”
外研社购书网址：https://fltrp.tmall.com

物料号：356620001

外国文学研究文库

前言

由北京外国语大学王佐良外国文学高等研究院策划、外语教学与研究出版社出版的“外国文学研究文库”就要与读者见面了。近年来，我国外国文学学界同仁一直在积极探索有效途径，引进国外学者的学术著作，以提升我国的学术研究水平，增强我国学者的国际学术话语权。但由于国外文学研究领域发展迅猛，以及国内出版经费缺乏等一系列问题，国外文学研究领域许多经典的和最新的研究成果无法得到及时传播与出版。为了弘扬我国老一辈学者外国文学研究的优秀传统，促进我国外国文学研究的深入开展，我们组织策划了这套“外国文学研究文库”，旨在将国外文学学界的学术成果及时引进和介绍给我国外国文学学者、学生及爱好者，反映外国文学研究领域在世界范围的发展趋势与前沿探索，使我国学界更好地与国际学界接轨与对话，以此推进我国外国文学研究的发展。

“外国文学研究文库”定位于对国外文学研究重要成果展开的

引介，将采用购买原作版权、组织国内该领域有影响的学者撰写导读的方式进行。这些导读将有助于读者把握作品的脉络，掌握其思想要点，更全面、更深入地理解作品要义。鉴于英语之外其他语种作品的受众问题，除以英语撰写的著作以原文的形式出版之外，我们拟将其他语种的国外学者著作翻译成汉语，并附以专家导读。该“文库”是一套开放性的系列丛书，我们将陆续推出国外具有影响力的学术著作，内容范围包括以下四个方向：外国文学理论、外国文学批评、比较文学理论与批评，以及文化批评研究。

北京外国语大学王佐良外国文学高等研究院邀请到了我国重要学者参加编委会，推荐挑选国外学界具有影响力的研究著作。国内这一领域的资深学者将为著作撰写导读，并为非英语著作确定译者。我们希望通过这套“文库”，为拓展和深化我国的外国文学研究，为帮助我国外国文学学者拓宽批评视野、开拓研究思路，尽我们的微薄之力。

这套“文库”的出版，得到了我国外国文学研究领域众多学者的鼎力相助和大力支持，也得到了外语教学与研究出版社的全力配合，特此表示衷心感谢！

金莉
北京外国语大学教授
王佐良外国文学高等研究院院长

走向共同文化

——《文化观念》导读

殷企平
杭州师范大学外国语学院

《文化观念》(*The Idea of Culture*，2000）出自伊格尔顿（Terry Eagleton，1943— ）之手。就文化批评而言，当今世界，无人能出其右。

早在 1998 年，牛津学者里甘（Stephen Regan）就称伊格尔顿为“当今最高产、最多才多艺的评论家”[1]。根据里甘的研究，“伊格尔顿是同辈中最具天赋的马克思主义思想家”，“没有任何其他文化批评家比他更受欢迎”，而且“他还凭一己之力，改造了批评话语的性质”[2]。时隔 20 多年以后，里甘的话仍然中肯。以文化为

1 Stephen Regan (ed.), *The Eagleton Reader* (Oxford: Blackwell, 1998), 封底。

2 Regan, *The Eagleton Reader*, p. viii.

题的著作浩如烟海，可是未见有人达到了伊格尔顿的高度。他迄今已有近 50 部专著问世，其中涉及文化理论的不在少数，不过从观念梳理的角度看，《文化观念》最值得称道——在文化观念史上，它堪称集大成之作。

初涉该书者，大都有“枝蔓丛生”的印象，一时摸不着方向。然而，细细品读之后，我们就会发现全书有一条主线，且始终围绕两大话题展开：1）文化陷入了何种危机？ 2）如何走出危机？全书共分五章，第一章“文化的不同说法”（“Versions of Culture”）可看作楔子，随及引出的第二章“危机中的文化”（“Culture in Crisis”）和第三章“文化战争”（“Culture Wars”）对应上述第一个话题，而第四章“文化与自然”（“Culture and Nature”）和第五章“走向共同文化”（“Towards a Common Culture”）则对应上述第二个话题。一言以蔽之，《文化观念》的诞生是为了应对当代文化危机。透过书中强烈的当下关怀，还可见一种深邃的历史视野。正因为如此，我们下面将从该书诞生的语境和背景说起。

一、《文化观念》诞生的语境和背景

在西方思想语境中，“文化”一词的含义有其逐渐展开与深化的过程，其基本脉络是从物质走向精神、从个体走向社会两种向度的延伸和转变。早在 18 世纪，欧洲的启蒙思想家就从社会变迁和历史发展的角度，直接或间接地论述了“文化”与“文明”这两个概念，以及它们在语义上既紧密联系又相互抵牾的关系。在英国，“文化”（culture）一词最早使用于 1420 年[1]，但其语义跟如今广为使用的“文化”不尽相同。不过，在 18 世纪之前的英国，文化观念虽还未正式形成，其内涵却早已处于孕育期，并经历了

1 “Culture,” in *Oxford English Dictionary*, 2nd ed. on CD-Rom (v.4.0) (Oxford: Oxford University Press, 2009).

漫长的萌芽 / 生发阶段，这在文学作品中尤为明显。[1]

也就是说，文化观念形成之前，其内涵早就萌发了，而且有一个逐渐走向成熟的过程；即使在成熟之后，也有一个不断扩展的趋势。这些丰富的内涵之一，便是对现代性的反思。[2] 作为一种文化传统，对现代性的反思至少可以追溯到 18 世纪。如戴维斯（Robert Con Davis）和施莱费尔（Ronald Schleifer）所说，18 世纪就已经存在一种"与启蒙理性'秩序'相对的文化秩序"[3]。但更确切地说，"文化"的种子早在资本主义萌芽时期就已经埋下，因而我们的视野将扩大到中世纪的一些作品，如《农夫皮尔斯》（*The Vision of Piers Plowman*，1370—1390）、《坎特伯雷故事集》（*The Canterbury Tales*，1387—1400）等——朦胧的文化意识早在那里就有迹可循了[4]。不过，文化观念本身则是在 19 世纪形成的。更具体地说，文化观念的牢固确立，有赖于卡莱尔（Thomas Carlyle，1795—1881）、阿诺德（Matthew Arnold，1822—1888）、罗斯金（John Ruskin，1819—1900）、金斯利（Charles Kingsley，1819—1875）和莫里斯（William Morris，1834—1896）等"维多利亚贤哲"（Victorian saints），正是他们"做了根基性的工作"[5]。通过他们的努力，"文化"一词越来越具有了针对现代文明的批判内涵（详见下文）。正因为如此，伊格尔顿在发表《文化观念》的十多年以后，还一直强调："'文化'一词直到 19 世

---

1 参见笔者作为总主编的《文化观念流变中的英国文学典籍研究》（6 卷本），上海：上海外语教育出版社，2020 年，总序。

2 参见拙著《"文化辩护书"：19 世纪英国文化批评》，上海：上海外语教育出版社，2013 年，第 1—2 页。

3 Robert Con Davis and Ronald Schleifer, *Literary Criticism: Literary and Cultural Studies* (New York: Longman, 1998), p. 322.

4 参见殷企平总主编：《文化观念流变中的英国文学典籍研究》（6 卷本），总序。

5 殷企平：《"文化辩护书"：19 世纪英国文化批评》，上海：上海外语教育出版社，2013 年，第 3 页。

纪才广泛流传。”[1]

在“维多利亚贤哲”和伊格尔顿之间，对文化观念史最有影响的要数威廉斯（Raymond Williams，1921—1988）。他的《文化与社会》（*Culture and Society: 1780-1950*，1958）和《漫长的革命》（*The Long Revolution*，1961）着眼于英国文学的文化主义传统研究，是迄今为止这方面首屈一指的经典之作。在《文化与社会》中，他首次指出：19 世纪思想史的一个重要产物是关于文化概念演变的假说，即“一个时期的艺术必然跟该时期普遍流行的‘生活方式’紧密相连，其结果是审美判断、道德判断和社会判断都互相紧密地联系在了一起”[2]。威廉斯的贡献在于，他率先勾勒了上述假说的形成轨迹，并对其背后的原因进行了鞭辟入里的分析。用他的原话说，“文化一词的演变记录了人们对历史性变化的反应，即对我们的社会、经济和政治生活中的重大历史性变化作出的重要而持续的反应。该词的演变本身好比一种特殊的地图，从中我们可以探索那些变化的性质”[3]。威廉斯此处所说的重大历史性变化，指的是社会转型，即农业文明向工业文明的转型，以及社会转型造成的社会、经济、政治乃至总体生活方式的空前变化。

威廉斯的另一个贡献是梳理文化观念的不同内涵。他在《关键词》（*Keywords: A Vocabulary of Culture and Society*，1976）一书中，从词源学的角度对“文化”一词含义的嬗变作过梳理。他尤为关注三种不同意义上的“文化”，即“艺术意义上的文化”（culture in the sense of the arts）、“作为美好生活品质的文化”（culture as civility）以及“社会生活意义上的文化”（culture in the sense of social life）。伊格尔顿肯定了威廉斯所作的上述区分，

---

1 Terry Eagleton, *Culture* (New Haven: Yale University Press, 2016), p. 10.

2 Raymond Williams, *Culture and Society: 1780-1950* (London: Chatto and Windus, 1958), p. 130.

3 Williams, *Culture and Society*, pp. xvi-xvii.

并赞赏他在指出这些词义变化的同时，看到了“一种思潮，即为连接不同意义上的文化而所作的努力”（20）。上述三种意义上的文化，彼此间确实存在着一种内在联系：艺术界定美好的生活品质，而后者需要政治变革——社会生活意义上的文化——来加以实现。这些文化语义上的变化，早已由阿诺德、罗斯金和莫里斯等人的文化实践和著述而促成，威廉斯所做的工作是加以记录、整理和提炼。

不过，伊格尔顿在肯定威廉斯所做工作的同时，也表达了他对后者的一个不满之处：“威廉斯撰写《关键词》时，虽记录了那些变化，但对其内在逻辑也许未保持足够的警觉。文化可指乌托邦批判，也可指生活方式，又可指艺术创造，是什么将它们联系起来的呢？答案肯定得从对文明的否定中去找：这三者都以各自的方式对实际文明作出了回应——文明标举人类自我发展的宏大叙事，却成就不了文化。”（20）此处所说的“乌托邦批判”，指的是把文化作为一种批判武器，其对象则是西方文明。伊格尔顿是在《文化观念》第一章“文化的不同说法”中说这番话的，这其实是挑明了自己写此书的动机之一，即超越文化观念史上的巨擘威廉斯。事实上，《文化观念》的最大优点也与此有关：批评威廉斯未能揭示上述文化语义变化的内在逻辑，这只是一个楔子，或只是表面原因，而更具深刻意义的是，伊格尔顿从中引出了一个重要观点，即在19世纪初，“文化观念开始从‘文明’的同义词转变成了它的反义词”（9），这其实是点出了文化观念成熟的时期和标志。[1]

如果说《文化观念》最重要的语境是文化语义的变化及其内在逻辑，那么它最重要的背景便是“文化”和“文明”的分家，也就是上文所暗示的逆转，即文化观念从“文明”的同义词转变成了它的反义词。用伊格尔顿自己的话说，“文化”和“文明”可谓

1 详见拙文《经由维多利亚文学的文化观念流变》，载《浙江外国语学院学报》2017年第5期。

同根同源，二者都“隶属于启蒙运动的总体精神”，只是到了19世纪，才发生了上述语义逆转。（9）在此之前，“文明”一词“集事实与价值于一身”（10），既标明某种社会生活形态，又隐含价值判断，如颂扬相关的生活形态及其精神诉求，或个人的全面发展、人际关系的和谐，以及国家的治理和昌盛等等。换言之，“文明”的语义原有两个基本层面，一是描述层面，二是规范层面；前者关乎事实，后者关乎价值。假如这一情况保持不变，那么“文化”就会跟“文明”亲如一家，二者就可以常被用来互换。然而，随着工业革命的兴起，“文明”的上述两个语义层面产生了分裂：它的描述/物质层面犹在，而它的规范/精神层面则丢失了，正如伊格尔顿后来所说，“文明如今只关乎事实，而文化却追问价值”[1]。言下之意，“文明”丢失的规范/精神层面，如今完全落在了“文化”身上，或者说，“文明”原有的价值使命，如今只能由“文化”来承担了。

应该说，揭示“文化”与“文明”分家的根本原因，这是《文化观念》的最大优点。不过，作者的写作动机远不止于此。除了针对“文明”而勾勒“文化”的根本性内涵之外，伊格尔顿还面临一个十分艰巨的任务：怎样走出文化在当代陷入的新危机？伊格尔顿所处的时代，可以用“文化热”来形容：人文社科领域，几乎没有一块未被“文化话语”冲击的地方。乍一看去，这似乎是一种喜人的现象，而且还有前文所说的“维多利亚贤哲”和威廉斯等人的影响。然而，凸显二律背反意味的新问题来了：“文化热”大潮之下，是五花八门的新理论、新话语——文化“吃香”，因而谁都想顶着它的名分。可想而知，这会带来很多问题，更糟糕的是会掩盖问题。诚如马海良先生所说，“‘文化热’隐含的内在矛盾”导致了“贯穿于现代时期”的“文化危机”，后者“表现

1 Eagleton, *Culture*, p. 10.

为现当代主流文化话语对文化的历史性、实践性、生产性以及政治性的漠视和掩盖”[1]。正是因为看到了这一问题，伊格尔顿忧心忡忡，下决心写作《文化观念》，以求化解危机，拨乱反正。

二、从“文化危机”到“文化战争”

《文化观念》第二章的标题就是“危机中的文化”。也就是在该章的第一段中，作者挑明了全书的核心观点：“本书的论点是：我们被夹在了两种文化观念的中间，一种大而无当，另一种僵化刻板，因而当务之急是两者都要超越。”（32）为什么会出现这一情况呢？

前文已经提到，由于文化“吃香”，因此谁都拿它当大旗，而当它指称一切时，自然就会变得空洞。关于这一点，不少研究伊格尔顿的学者都已经发表了见解，其中以马海良先生的阐释最为简明：“现代‘文化’概念从替换‘文明’开始，一路不断繁殖，到后现代主义时期膨胀成为包揽一切的最高能指，伊格尔顿称之为‘唯文化论’或‘文化主义’（culturalism）。当‘文化’成为一个无所不能容纳的概念时，也就成了一个大而无当的没有意义内涵的空洞符号。”[2] 不无悖论意义的是，此处所说的“包揽一切”往往走向其反面：各路话语都顶着“文化”的名头，看似后者包揽了一切，实则此文化非彼文化，每一种“文化”都很狭窄。这就是上引文字中“文化主义”的要害所在，或者说后现代主义的要害所在。这一点已由刘静和冯伟说得很清楚：“进入后现代，文化以无所不在的方式成为一种独特的存在……后现代主义是一种文化主义，首先是因为它拒绝承认不同种族在社会上和经济上所

1 马海良：《伊格尔顿批评理论的文化主题》，载《文艺理论研究》2014 年第 2 期，第 113 页。

2 马海良：《伊格尔顿批评理论的文化主题》，第 116 页。

共有的东西比文化差异更为重要。而正是这些东西关乎着政治解放。后现代的偏见不断地腐蚀、破坏作为对文明的批评的文化。文化概念作为批评或乌托邦的维度迅速地衰落。”[1] 换言之，“‘文化’由曾经俯瞰和统辖整个人间事务的第一原子分裂为‘不同的’差异性形态，‘文化’裂变为‘各种文化’”[2]，这是当年阿诺德乃至威廉斯等人都未曾料到的新问题。

应该说，上述新问题——文化危机——产生的原因很复杂。除已经提到的外，“文化”一词本身的特殊性也是重要原因之一。就像很多学者指出的那样，“文化”是“英语语言中两三个最复杂的单词之一”，而且“很少有比‘文化’更成问题的词语了”[3]。从词源学的角度看，它历经千变万化，最终“把马克思所说的经济基础与上层建筑统一在了单个概念之中”（1—2）。换言之，“文化”一词经过长时期的演变，派生出了许多复杂的内涵和外延。更复杂的是，它最初的语义就呈复合态势，而且是复合了二元对立的内涵：“如果文化最初的意义是耕作，那么它既暗示着规范，又暗示着自然生长。”（4）随着语义演变的深入，这种二元对立的趋势也愈演愈烈，就如伍晓明所说，文化观念包含了“一系列二元对立的解构”[4]。正因为如此，《文化观念》从篇首就开始分析“文化”一词的二元对立式含义——这些含义成双成对，却又互相矛盾。略举数端如下：

---

1 刘静、冯伟：《摆正文化的位置——伊格尔顿的文化观探析》，载《理论月刊》2018 年第 2 期，第 38—39 页。

2 马海良：《伊格尔顿批评理论的文化主题》，第 116 页。

3 分别参见 Raymond Williams, *Keywords: A Vocabulary of Culture and Society*, Flamingo: Fontana, 1983, p. 87；Patrick Fuery and Nick Mansfield, *Cultural Studies and the New Humanities: Concepts and Controversies*, Melbourne: Oxford University Press, 1997, p. xviii；以及本书第 1 页。

4 伍晓明：《论伊格尔顿的文化观》，载《浙江社会科学》2020 年第 4 期，第 122 页。

乡村生活（rural existence）	vs	城市生活（urban existence)
自然生长（natural growth）	vs	约束管理（regulation）
养猪业（pig-farming）	vs	毕加索艺术（Picasso）
耕种土地（tilling the soil）	vs	分裂原子（splitting the atom）
制作（making）	vs	被制作（being made）
率性（spontaneity）	vs	理性（rationality）
自我实现（self-realization）	vs	自我克服（self-overcoming）
高级官能（higher faculties）	vs	低级官能（lower faculties）
实际形成的（what has actually evolved）	vs	应该形成的（what ought to evolve）

（1—6）

以上列表只反映了文化观念丰富内涵中的一小部分，不过它们具有代表性。伊格尔顿所分析的内涵都具有二元性，或者如他自己所说的“两面性”（facing both ways）:“文化作为一个词语具有两面性。它还暗示我们自身内部就可分成两个部分，一部分行使培养和冶炼的功能，而另一部分则构成了供冶炼的原材料。”（5）此处所说“行使培养和冶炼的功能”就是上表中的“高级官能”，而“供冶炼的原材料”则是与之对应的“低级官能”。

正是因为上述烦冗驳杂的语义内涵，“文化”一词即便暂时不受历史、社会语境变化的影响，也会因其内在张力（不同乃至相反的语义彼此互动或博弈）而处于一种动态之中。更确切地说，“文化”一词从一开始就蕴含着不调和的种子。面对这些不调和的种子，伊格尔顿立下了两大功劳：1）从错综复杂的线索中理出了一个具有共性的头绪，即（如上文所暗示的那样）众多语义彼此间都有一种对立统一的辩证关系；2）在扑朔迷离的线索中导出主线，即勾勒出了“文化”与“文明”分道扬镳的轨迹（参见本文第一小节的最后三段）。然而，理出这些头绪 / 主线并不能让人一劳永逸。伊格尔顿清楚地看到，“文化”概念并非生活在真空当中，它的“每一次使用都反映了历史语境对‘意义’的调整需求”[1]。由于前文所述的新历史语境，即各路话语 / 理论争相标举“文化”大旗的情境，因此出现了新的文化危机[2]，其“征兆表现为对历史条件的掩盖、意图与效果的冲突和自我涂写与抹除的矛盾”[3]。这一新的历史条件，反过来会激活我们所说“不调和的种子”——虽然各类理论都标举“文化”，但是每类理论（以及操弄理论的各种势力）其实有不同的文化认同，或者说只认同了文化观念众多内涵中的某些部分，那就必然会带来新的“不调和”。正是在这一意义上，笔者认同韩伟和徐蔚两位学者对《文化观念》的解读，即“文化的危机是文化认同的危机”[4]。可能也正是因为看到了这一点，伊格尔顿才在第一章中大书特书“文化的不同说法”，以此为其后讲危机的两章作铺垫，进而为最后一章（讲如何走出危机）埋下伏笔，也就是为全书奠定基础。

上述危机一直呈愈演愈烈的趋势，以致伊格尔顿只能专辟一章（第三章），并冠以“文化战争”的标题，来显示其激烈程度。该章开宗明义：“‘文化战争’这个短语暗示混战，即民粹主义者与精英主义者之战、经典监护人与**差异**[5]信奉者之战，以及已故白种男性[6]与被不公平地边缘化者之间的白热战。”（51）此处须特别留意的是“差异”一词：参加混战的“文化斗士”其实是各自为战、

1 马海良：《伊格尔顿批评理论的文化主题》，第 115 页。

2 笔者此处之所以用了“新的文化危机”，是因为文化史上其实危机不断。伊格尔顿本人也承认，“宣称文化观念如今正处于危机之中，这是很危险的，因为它何时不在危机之中呢？”（37）。

3 马海良：《伊格尔顿批评理论的文化主题》，第 115 页。

4 韩伟、徐蔚：《文化的危机与弥合——读伊格尔顿的〈文化的观念〉》，载《文艺评论》2010 年第 1 期，第 11 页。

5 原文 difference 为斜体，故译文用粗体与之相对应。

6 “已故白种男性”原文为 dead white males，常用来暗讽占据经典地位的都是些男性白种人，而且都已过世，亦即喻其性别歧视、种族歧视和僵化过时。

各为其“主”（各自不同的文化主张）。用韩伟和徐蔚的话来说，伊格尔顿敏锐地发现“各个阶层、各个民族对文化理解的差异导致了文化和政治的对抗”[1]。当然，导致这种混战的还有不同性别对文化理解的差异，甚至有不同性取向者之间的差异——上引文字中的“被不公平地边缘化者”（the unjustly marginalized）就包括了女权主义者和“酷儿理论”（Queer Theory）的拥趸。显然，这些不同的文化主张已经被注入了政治含义，或者说已经被政治化了。

使上述情形更为复杂化的是，伊格尔顿还发现“文化战争”不仅发生在不同性别、阶级和种族之间，而且发生在“大写文化”（Culture）与“小写文化”（culture）之间。所谓“小写文化”，指的是某一种具体的文化形态，如女权主义文化、精英主义文化等。至于“大写文化”，伊格尔顿第一次在书中使用它时，称其为“浪漫主义、前马克思主义的名称，意在批判早期工业资本主义”（10）。在其后的阐释中，伊格尔顿又强调“大写文化”其实就相当于传统意义上的“文化”（culture），而“小写文化”则相当于“一种文化”（a culture），前者是比后者“更博大的、无所不包的形态”（38）。这种博大而无所不包的“大写文化”跟当年阿诺德等人的文化理想相吻合，其初衷是超越一切，超越任何狭隘的阶级、种族、性别和宗派利益，也就是超越任何“一种文化”。可惜事与愿违，它不幸沦落到了无法对任何“一种文化”言说的境地，难怪伊格尔顿又称其为“无文化可言”（cultureless）：“大写文化的问题是它竟无文化可言：它的价值观不为任何具体生活形态所采纳；干脆地说，不为人类的任何实际生活所采纳。”（53）假如这一问题仅仅停留在学术层面，那么它还不至于成为燃眉之急，但是在当今世界，它已然成为一个严峻的现实问题：

1 韩伟、徐蔚：《文化的危机与弥合——读伊格尔顿的〈文化的观念〉》，第11页。

> 然而，大写文化与小写文化之间的争执，不再仅仅是一场有关定义的争战，而且是一种全球性的冲突。它事关现实政治，而不只牵涉学术。它不单单是司汤达与《塞恩菲尔德》之间的争斗[1]，也不仅仅是在英语系走廊上研究弥尔顿诗歌尾韵的那些家伙与专写手淫的那些聪明年轻人之间的争吵[2]，而是新千年世界政治格局的组成部分。我们将会看到，就政治而言，尽管文化不是至高无上的，但是它却与我们的世界息息相关——在这个世界上，三个最富有者的财富相当于六亿个赤贫者财富的总和。文化战争关注的是种族清洗这类问题，而不是拉辛[3]与肥皂剧孰优孰劣这样的问题，因而是非常要紧的。（51）

伊格尔顿此处用了“要紧”一词，这说明他虽然把“文化战争”看作一种“混战”（详见本段的上文），却很重视其关注的现实问题，或者说他也要解决这些问题，并视之为文化所面临的新任务。有趣的是，他把文化承担新任务这一现象描绘为“文化膨胀”（the inflation of culture）：“文化膨胀是世俗化时代故事的一部分，就像文学那样——自阿诺德以降，它居然率先承担起了伦理、思想乃至政治方面的重任！这些任务先前是由更偏重技术和实用的话语来承担的。”（40）须说明的是，此处的“文化膨胀”与前文所

1 司汤达（Stendhal，1783—1842），原名 Marie-Henri Beyle，法国著名小说家，《红与黑》等的作者；《塞恩菲尔德》，又译《宋飞传》，美国全国广播公司播出的广受欢迎的情景喜剧，由好莱坞知名喜剧演员塞恩菲尔德（Jerome Allen “Jerry” Seinfeld，1954— ）饰演半自传的同名剧中角色。伊格尔顿用这两者来代表经典艺术与通俗艺术之争。

2 “聪明年轻人”原文为 bright young things，可直译为“聪明而年轻的东西”，含讥讽的意味。

3 拉辛（Jean Racine，1639—1699），法国著名剧作家、诗人。

说“文化”概念的膨胀（即变成包揽一切的最高能指）既有联系又有不同，后者侧重概念内涵的过度扩张，而前者则强调文化承担的各类新任务，包括政治任务。

我们不妨把上述现象称为文化的“政治转向”。用伊格尔顿的话说，“文化已经具有了一种新的政治重要性”（131）。从伊格尔顿的总体思想来看，他是认可这种转向的，但他同时又面临如下困境：在名目林立的文化理论中，有没有一种理论能脱颖而出，引导世人既真正承担起政治重任，又不至于陷入上述混战呢？我们将在下一小节对接这一话题。

三、走向共同文化

该怎样走出上述文化危机（“文化战争”只是它的一种激烈形式）呢？根据伊格尔顿的分析，“小写文化”显然是无能为力的，那么“大写文化”呢？前文提到，“大写文化”志在超越任何阶级、种族、性别和宗派的狭隘利益，但是它同样无所作为。用伊格尔顿的原话来说就是：“大写文化之所以拯救不了我们，是因为它其实并不认为自己受历史条件限制，因而也就无权过问人间烟火（has no title to intervene in sublunary affairs）。”（86）此处所谓“不受历史条件限制”，就是马海良先生所说的“现当代主流文化话语对文化的历史性、实践性、生产性以及政治性的漠视和掩盖”（详见本文第一小节尾部），而这一状况的“根源在于资本主义制度的固有矛盾”[1]。既然“大写文化”无所作为的根源在于资本主义，那么要走出文化危机，还是要从批判资本主义入手，而伊格尔顿的思路也是这样展开的。这一点在刘静和冯伟的笔下有较好的解读：

1 马海良：《伊格尔顿批评理论的文化主题》，第 113 页。

> 威廉斯时期文化的政治正在演变为文化政治，进而可能堕入文化取代政治的意识形态陷阱。面对这种理论迷失，伊格尔顿始终保持着清醒的头脑，批判文化主义和文化相对主义的种种弊端，揭示后现代资本主义社会中文化的地位和作用，指出文化在后现代的过度膨胀掩盖了其无力的表现。在他看来，文化不足以作为政治的替代来行使政治批评功能，文化的自大具有严重的后果，摆正文化的位置成为当今理论研究刻不容缓的任务。[1]

值得留意的是，上引文字中有“文化的自大”一语。确实，伊格尔顿在《文化观念》的结尾处就是这么说的。我们前面已经引用了该书的倒数第三句，即“文化已经具有了一种新的政治重要性”，而其后的两句是这样写的：“但是它同时也变得傲慢与自负了。在承认它具有意义的同时，是我们把它放回本位的时候了。”（131）此言一出，引起了很多反响，不过最多的是一种误读——很多人的解读是：文化已经变得不那么重要了。情况果真如此吗？

诚然，把文化的“傲慢与自负”放在全书最后的位置，这似乎是要铁板钉钉，至少是语出惊人。然而，我们仍须问一句：这话是针对什么讲的，是在什么语境下讲的？首先，它是作为第五章（也是作为全书）的结束语讲的，而这一章的标题是“走向共同文化”。就行文逻辑而论，起点题作用的自然是相关章节的题目，而该章居于最后位置的语句自然是要为所在章节题目服务的。进一步说，“走向共同文化”作为《文化观念》全书的最后一章，其重要地位不言自喻，那么它的最后两句——“但是它同时也变得傲慢与自负了。在承认它具有意义的同时，是我们把它放回本位的时候了”——必然是服务于全章中心论点的，即提倡共同文化。

1 刘静、冯伟：《摆正文化的位置——伊格尔顿的文化观探析》，第 37 页。

换言之，“共同文化”与“傲慢自负的文化”之间形成了一种张力，其间正是众多关于文化的“不同说法”及其相关危机 / 混战。这一形式上的张力本身就在传达一个信息，即共同文化将要战胜自大的文化，从而走出全书所分析的文化危机。从行文手段来看，另一个文本细节也值得推敲：上引“变得傲慢与自负”一句其实又受到了其后（即最后）一句的限定——作者主张把文化“放回本位”，而这放回本位的文化就是共同文化，是与自大的文化相对立的。不仅如此，限制“变得傲慢与自负”这一句的还有其上文——同一段的首句和第二句是这样写的：“文化是我们赖以生活的一切。在很大程度上，它还是我们为之生活的一切。”（131）还有比这更强调文化重要性的吗？

由此可见，伊格尔顿在书尾提出“傲慢自负的文化”一说，丝毫没有贬低文化重要性的意思。那么，他为什么要那样说呢？学界炒作“傲慢自负的文化”一说的人还常常拿伊格尔顿的另一本书《文化》（*Culture*，2016）说事，该书的结语部分有一个小标题，就叫作“文化的傲慢”（“The Hubris of Culture”）。事实上，这一标题是有歧义的。我们应该细究的是，伊格尔顿是在说文化本身的傲慢呢，还是某些文化工作者的傲慢？抑或是某种文化理论及其拥趸的傲慢？不妨来看一下《文化》的具体文字。在以“文化的傲慢”为题的结语中，伊格尔顿一上来就说：“文学批评家一直对自己的重要性存疑。”[1] 此处的“文学批评家”主要指教授文化知识的大学教师，他们对自己的重要性都存疑，难道会傲慢吗？紧跟着上一句，伊格尔顿又说：“文学应对的是人类现实中最根本的问题，这是不可否认的。”[2] 这分明强调了文化——文学是文化的核心部分——的重要性，那么“傲慢”又从何谈起呢？到了第三句，

1 Eagleton, *Culture*, p. 149.

2 Eagleton, *Culture*, p. 149.

我们才看明白："自从文学作品的研究抛弃了公共领域，躲进了学术界，它就成了次要活动，这种边缘化的程度使人不难想象大学文学系正在成为明日黄花（确实，整个艺术人文学科都如此）。"[1] 原来伊格尔顿是在批评那些抛弃了公共领域的艺术人文学科工作者！伊格尔顿用上述三句话，揭示了一个具有悖论意义的现象：一方面，许多文化工作者"躲在象牙塔里，无视普通读者，不屑于构建公共领域"[2]，因而他们是傲慢的；另一方面，他们又是孤独的、缺乏自信的——由于他们躲在了象牙塔里，因此就会陷入孤立，自然也就有了"对自己的重要性都存疑"一说。

《文化》中批判的"傲慢"，早在《文化观念》中就遭到批判了。前文述及的各类"小写文化"大都有傲慢的毛病，躲在象牙塔里，不屑于构建公共领域。它们之所以陷入混战，是因为它们拒绝承认"共有的东西比文化差异更为重要"（详见本文第二小节第二段和第五段）。作为一个有人类大同理想的马克思主义者，伊格尔顿必然想超越导致文化危机 / 战争的差异，必然要寻求走出危机的文化策略。那么，貌似具有超越性的"大写文化"是否可行呢？遗憾的是，它也无济于事，其原因是它"不食人间烟火"，或者说"并不认为自己受历史条件限制"（参见本小节第一段）。须顺带提一句：不食人间烟火，也是一种傲慢。

正是鉴于"大写文化"和"小写文化"都难有作为的情况，伊格尔顿把目光投向了共同文化。作为一个术语，"共同文化"是威廉斯首先提出来的。后者在 1958 年分别发表论文《文化是普通的》（"Culture Is Ordinary"）和专著《文化与社会》，里面都阐述了他的共同文化观。在《文化是普通的》一文中，他这样说道："在下半个世纪中，我们社会的核心问题是如何使用新资源

1 Eagleton, *Culture*, p. 149.

2 李睿、殷企平：《"共同体"与外国文学研究——殷企平教授访谈录》，载《复旦外国语言文学论丛》2021 年第 2 期，第 62—63 页。

来营造一种良性的共同文化。”[1] 在《文化与社会》中，上述“核心问题”更凸显出迫切性，被摆在了人类生死存亡的高度：“我们需要一种共同文化，不是为了有一个抽象原则，而是因为没有它，我们就无法生存。”[2] 在威廉斯看来，共同文化跟“共同体”（community）、“沟通交流”（communication）和思想 / 知识的“传播”（transmission）息息相关：

> ……传播永远是一种奉献……它不是要控制，而是要沟通，是要让人采纳和响应。人们是否积极采纳你所传播的东西，是否踊跃响应，则取决于是否有一个有效的体验共同体。可以肯定，这种交流的质量又取决于人们是否认可实际的平等。形形色色的不平等分裂了我们的社会，从而使人们很难有效地沟通交流，甚至无法交流。[3]

上引文字中的“体验共同体”（community of experience）显然强调了文化实践的物质性、历史性和普遍性，或者说体现了马克思主义的历史唯物主义思想。有意思的是，伊格尔顿从中找到了共同文化的成因和立足依据。《文化观念》第四章“文化与自然”的结尾是这样写的：

> 一种共同文化之所以能够形成，只是因为我们的身体大致属于相同的种类，因而一种共性有赖于另一种共性。就像马克思在青年时期所意识到的那样，即便是我们在作为个体时，身体也带有社会烙印，而且比文化的

1 Raymond Williams, “Culture Is Ordinary”, in *The Raymond Williams Reader*, ed. John Higgins (Oxford: Blackwell, 2001), p. 17.

2 Williams, *Culture and Society*, p. 336.

3 Williams, *Culture and Society*, p. 336.

> 烙印更深。当然，人的身体因历史、性别、种族和体能等方面的不同而不同，但是他们在语言、劳动和性征等方面的性能则没有区别，这些性能使他们一开始就进入了一种彼此相连的关系，一种具有潜在共性的关系。后现代主义者鼓吹人的身体是后天构造而成的，这已经成了一种迷信。狂热崇拜这一观点的人虽然在批判先天论时显得很聪明，却与放弃抵抗资本主义的那些人沆瀣一气——他们抛弃的是与资本主义进行全球性对抗的政治观，而这恰恰发生在一个资本主义寻求全球性霸权的时代，一个全球性霸权政治比以往任何时候都更咄咄逼人的时代。（111）

这段文字表明，共同文化赖以立足的基础是人的自然属性。前文提到，后现代文化理论的拥趸是否定人类自然属性 / 共性的，他们眼里只有差异和个性，根本看不到人类在身体构造、语言、劳动和性征等方面的共性。假如他们的谬见只停留在学术定义层面，那么其危害性还不至于很严重，但是他们正好跟资本主义的全球性政治霸权形成了一种共谋关系，因此已经到了非反抗不可的地步。伊格尔顿敏锐地捕捉到了问题的症结，从而提出了建设共同文化的目标，并为此奠定了理论基础，可谓功莫大焉。还得顺带提一句：在本文引言部分，笔者把《文化观念》第四章和第五章一并对应于“如何走出危机”这一话题，这种对应关系由本段论述可见一斑。更确切地说，第四章为第五章中提出“共同文化”做了准备。

还须一提的是，虽然伊格尔顿的“共同文化”说得益于威廉斯，但是他并未停留在同一水平。这一点已经由马海良先生点明：“伊格尔顿更进一步的地方在于，他借用马克思的经济生产理论，以文学生产为个案，提出别具新意的文化生产理论。文化的历史性、物质性和实践性在伊格尔顿的理论建构中被综合描述为一种‘生产性’。”[1] 换言之，“历史唯物主义的生产方式理论是他谋求走出文化危机的可靠资源；在他看来，直至今天的文化危机，其最大的根源是资本主义的整体生产方式及其文化生产方式”，而“解决文化危机的关键是解决文化生产资料所有权的问题，推行社会主义的物质实践”[2]。我们还须补充一点：伊格尔顿比威廉斯更进一步的地方，还在于他把“趣味”元素揉进了共同文化理论。下面这段论述可以为证：

> 威廉斯的共同文化理论……不会受到激进主义杂糅论者和自由主义多元论者无保留的欢迎，这是因为它必然需要一种信仰和行动的公共性，而这几乎是不合他们趣味的。威廉斯的立场是一个悖论：这种复杂的文化发展的条件，只有通过在政治上确保某种手段才能设定——他把后者相当含糊地称作“共同体手段”，而实际上他指的就是社会主义的公共机构。这样做就肯定需要公共的信仰、承诺和实践。只有通过充分的民主参与，包括调节物质生产的民主制度，才能充分开放表达这种文化多元性的通道。简而言之，要确立真正的文化多元主义，就需要齐心协力的社会主义行动。当代文化主义未能明白的，恰恰是这一要点。（121—122）

由此可见，伊格尔顿把“趣味”（见上面引文第四行）等同于“信仰和行动的公共性”，或者说“社会主义行动”所体现的“齐心协

1 马海良：《伊格尔顿批评理论的文化主题》，第 117 页。

2 马海良：《伊格尔顿批评理论的文化主题》，第 118 页。

力”，也就是他在许多著述中强调的“公共精神”[1]。正是这种公共精神，构成了共同文化的精髓。

《文化观念》发表于20多年前，可是它如今读来仍然非常亲切。谓其亲切，是因为文化危机仍然存在，文化战争仍然硝烟弥漫，资本主义全球性霸权仍在作祟，而共同文化仍不失为最佳解药。

1 参见拙文《走向公共精神：伊格尔顿的趣味观》，载《外国文学》2022年第6期，第79页。

The Idea of Culture

For Edward Said

Contents

1

Versions of Culture

'Culture' is said to be one of the two or three most complex words in the English language, and the term which is sometimes considered to be its opposite – nature – is commonly awarded the accolade of being the most complex of all. Yet though it is fashionable these days to see nature as a derivative of culture, culture, etymologically speaking, is a concept derived from nature. One of its original meanings is 'husbandry', or the tending of natural growth. The same is true of our words for law and justice, as well as of terms like 'capital', 'stock', 'pecuniary' and 'sterling'. The word 'coulter', which is a cognate of 'culture', means the blade of a ploughshare. We derive our word for the finest of human activities from labour and agriculture, crops and cultivation. Francis Bacon writes of 'the culture and manurance of minds', in a suggestive hesitancy between dung and mental distinction. 'Culture' here means an activity, and it was a long time before the word came to denote an entity. Even then, it was probably not until Matthew Arnold that the word dropped such adjectives as 'moral' and 'intellectual' and came to be just 'culture', an abstraction in itself.

Etymologically speaking, then, the now-popular phrase 'cultural materialism' is something of a tautology. 'Culture' at first denoted a thoroughly material process, which was then metaphorically transposed to affairs of the spirit. The word thus charts within its semantic unfolding humanity's own historic shift from rural to urban existence, pig-farming to Picasso, tilling the soil to splitting the atom. In Marxist parlance, it brings together both base and superstructure in a single notion. Perhaps behind the pleasure we are supposed to take in 'cultivated' people lurks a race-memory of drought and famine. But the semantic shift is also paradoxical: it is the urban dwellers who are 'cultivated', and those who actually live by tilling the soil who are not. Those who cultivate the land are less able to cultivate themselves. Agriculture leaves no leisure for culture.

The Latin root of the word 'culture' is *colere*, which can mean anything from cultivating and inhabiting to worshipping and protecting. Its meaning as 'inhabit' has evolved from the Latin *colonus* to the contemporary 'colonialism', so that titles like *Culture and Colonialism* are, once again, mildly tautological. But *colere* also ends up via the Latin *cultus* as the religious term 'cult', just as the idea of culture itself in the modern age comes to substitute itself for a fading sense of divinity and transcendence. Cultural truths – whether high art or the traditions of a people – are sometimes sacred ones, to be protected and revered. Culture, then, inherits the imposing mantle of religious authority, but also has uneasy affinities with occupation and invasion; and it is between these two poles, positive and negative, that the concept is currently pitched. It is one of those rare ideas which have been as integral to the political left as they are vital to the political right, and its social history is thus exceptionally tangled and ambivalent.

If the word 'culture' traces a momentous historical transition, it also encodes a number of key philosophical issues. Within this single term, questions of freedom and determinism, agency and endurance, change and identity, the given and the created, come dimly into focus. If culture means the active tending of natural growth, then it suggests a dialectic between the artificial and the natural, what we do to the world and what the world does to us. It is an epistemologically 'realist' notion, since it implies that there is a nature or raw material beyond ourselves; but it also has a 'constructivist' dimension, since this raw material must be worked up into humanly significant shape. So it is less a matter of deconstructing the opposition between culture and nature than of recognizing that the term 'culture' is already such a deconstruction.

In a further dialectical turn, the cultural means we use to transform nature are themselves derived from it. The point is made rather more poetically by Polixenes in Shakespeare's *The Winter's Tale*:

> Yet nature is made better by no mean
> But nature makes that mean; so over that art,
> Which you say adds to nature, is an art
> That nature makes . . . This is an art
> Which does mend nature – change it rather, but
> The art itself is nature.
>
> (Act IV, sc. iv)

Nature produces culture which changes nature: it is a familiar motif of the so-called Last Comedies, which see culture as the medium of nature's constant self-refashioning. If Ariel in *The Tempest* is all airy agency and Caliban all earthy inertia, a more dialectical interplay of culture and nature can be found in Gonzalo's description of Ferdinand swimming from the wrecked ship:

> Sir, he may live;
> I saw him beat the surges under him,
> And ride upon their backs; he trod the water,
> Whose enmity he flung aside, and breasted
> The surge most swoln that met him; his bold head
> 'Bove the contentious waves he kept, and oared
> Himself with his good arms in lusty stroke
> To th' shore . . .
>
> (Act II, sc. i)

Swimming is an apt image of the interplay in question, since the swimmer actively creates the current which sustains him, plying the waves so they may return to buoy him up. Thus Ferdinand 'beats the surges' only to 'ride upon their backs', treads, flings, breasts and oars an ocean which is by no means just pliable material but 'contentious', antagonistic, recalcitrant to human shaping. But it is just this resistance which allows him to act upon it. Nature itself produces the means of its own transcendence, rather as the Derridean 'supplement' is already contained by whatever it amplifies. As we shall see later, there is something oddly necessary about the gratuitous superabundance we call culture. If nature is always in some sense cultural, then cultures are built out of that ceaseless traffic with nature which we call labour. Cities are raised out of sand, wood, iron, stone, water and the like, and are thus quite as natural as rural idylls are cultural. The geographer David Harvey argues that there is nothing 'unnatural' about New York city, and doubts that tribal peoples can be said to be 'closer to nature' than the West.[1] The word 'manufacture' originally means handicraft, and is thus 'organic', but comes over time to denote mechanical mass production, and so picks up a pejorative overtone of artifice, as in 'manufacturing divisions where none exist'.

If culture originally means husbandry, it suggests both regulation and spontaneous growth. The cultural is what we can change, but the stuff to be altered has its own autonomous existence, which then lends it something of the recalcitrance of nature. But culture is also a matter of following rules, and this too involves an interplay of the regulated and unregulated. To follow a rule is not like obeying a physical law, since it involves a creative application of the rule in question. 2–4–6–8–10–30 may well represent a rule-bound sequence, just not the rule one most expects. And there can be no rules for applying rules, under pain of infinite regress. Without such open-endedness, rules would not be rules, rather as words would not be words; but this does not mean that any move whatsoever can count as following a rule. Rule-following is a matter neither of anarchy nor autocracy. Rules, like cultures, are neither sheerly random nor rigidly determined – which is to say that both involve the idea of freedom. Someone who was entirely absolved from cultural conventions would be no more free than someone who was their slave.

The idea of culture, then, signifies a double refusal: of organic determinism on the one hand, and of the autonomy of spirit on the other. It is a rebuff to both naturalism and idealism, insisting against the former that there is that within nature which exceeds and undoes it, and against idealism that even the most high-minded human agency has its humble roots in our biology and natural environment. The fact that culture (like nature in this respect) can be both a descriptive and evaluative term, meaning what has actually evolved as well as what ought to, is relevant to this refusal of both naturalism and idealism. If the concept sets its face against determinism, it is equally wary of voluntarism. Human beings are not mere products of their environs, but neither are those environs sheer clay for their arbitrary self-fashioning. If culture transfigures nature, it is a project to which nature sets rigorous limits. The very word 'culture' contains a tension between making and being made, rationality and spontaneity, which upbraids the disembodied intellect of the Enlightenment as much as it defies the cultural reductionism of so much contemporary thought. It even hints towards the political contrast between evolution and revolution – the former 'organic' and 'spontaneous', the latter artificial and *voulu* – and suggests how one might move beyond this stale antithesis too. The word oddly commingles growth and calculation, freedom and necessity, the idea of a conscious project but also of an unplannable surplus. And if this is true of the word, so is it of some of the activities it denotes. When Friedrich Nietzsche looked for a practice which might dismantle the opposition between freedom and determinism, it was to the experience of making art that he turned, which for the artist feels not only free *and* necessary, creative *and* constrained, but each of these in terms of the other, and so appears to press these rather tattered old polarities to the point of undecidability.

There is another sense in which culture as a word faces both ways. For it can also suggest a division within ourselves, between that part of us which cultivates and refines, and whatever within us constitutes the raw material for such refinement. Once culture is grasped as *self*-culture, it posits a duality between higher and lower faculties, will and desire, reason and passion, which it then instantly offers to overcome. Nature now is not just the stuff of the world, but the dangerously appetitive stuff of the self. Like culture, the word means both what is around us and inside us, and the disruptive drives within can easily be equated with anarchic forces without. Culture is thus a matter of self-overcoming as much as self-realization. If it celebrates the self, it also disciplines it, aesthetic and ascetic together. Human nature is not quite the same as a field of beetroot, but like a field it needs to be cultivated – so that as the word 'culture' shifts us from the natural to the spiritual, it also intimates an affinity between them. If we are cultural beings, we are also part of the nature on which we go to work. Indeed it is part of the point of the word 'nature' to remind us of the continuum between ourselves and our surroundings, just as the word 'culture' serves to highlight the difference.

In this process of self-shaping, action and passivity, the strenuously willed and the sheerly given, unite once more, this time in the same individuals. We resemble nature in that we, like it, are to be cuffed into shape, but we differ from it in that we can do this to ourselves, thus introducing into the world a degree of self-reflexivity to which the rest of nature cannot aspire. As self-cultivators, we are clay in our own hands, at once redeemer and unregenerate, priest and sinner in the same body. Left to its own devices, our reprobate nature will not spontaneously rise to the grace of culture; but neither can such grace be rudely forced upon it. It must rather cooperate with the innate tendencies of nature itself, in order to induce it to transcend itself. Like grace, culture must already represent a potential within human nature, if it is to stick. But the very need for culture suggests that there is something lacking in nature – that our capacity to rise to heights beyond those of our fellow natural creatures is necessary because our natural condition is also a good deal more 'unnatural' than that of our fellows. If there is a history and a politics concealed in the word 'culture', there is also a theology.

Cultivation, however, may not only be something we do to ourselves. It may also be something done to us, not least by the political state. For the state to flourish, it must inculcate in its citizens the proper sorts of spiritual disposition; and it is this which the idea of culture or *Bildung* signifies in a venerable tradition from Schiller to Matthew Arnold.[2] In civil society, individuals live in a state of chronic antagonism, driven by opposing interests; but the state is that transcendent realm in which these divisions can be harmoniously reconciled. For this to happen, however, the state must already have been at work in civil society, soothing its rancour and refining its sensibilities; and this process is what we know as culture. Culture is a kind of ethical pedagogy which will fit us for political citizenship by liberating the ideal or collective self buried within each of us, a self which finds supreme representation in the universal realm of the state. Coleridge writes accordingly of the need to ground civilization in cultivation, 'in the harmonious development of those qualities and faculties that characterise our *humanity*. We must be men in order to be citizens'.[3] The state incarnates culture, which in turn embodies our common humanity.

To elevate culture over politics – to be men first and citizens later – means that politics must move within a deeper ethical dimension, drawing on the resources of *Bildung* and forming individuals into suitably well-tempered, responsible citizens. This is the rhetoric of the civics class, if a little more highly pitched. But since 'humanity' here means a community free of conflict, what is at stake is not just the priority of culture over politics, but over a particular kind of politics. Culture, or the state, are a sort of premature utopia, abolishing struggle at an imaginary level so that they need not resolve it at a political one. Nothing could be less politically innocent than a denigration of politics in the name of the human. Those who proclaim the need for a period of ethical incubation to prepare men and women for political citizenship include those who deny colonial peoples the right to self-government until they are 'civilized' enough to exercise it responsibly. They overlook the fact that by far the best preparation of political independence is political independence. Ironically, then, a case which moves from humanity to culture to politics betrays by its own political bias the fact that the real movement is the other way – that it is political interests which usually govern cultural ones, and in doing so define a particular version of humanity.

What culture does, then, is distil our common humanity from our sectarian political selves, redeeming the spirit from the senses, wresting the changeless from the temporal, and plucking unity from diversity. It signifies a kind of self-division as well as a self-healing, by which our fractious, sublunary selves are not abolished, but refined from within by a more ideal sort of humanity. The rift between state and civil society – between how the bourgeois citizen would like to represent himself and how he actually is – is preserved but also eroded. Culture is a form of universal subjectivity at work within each of us, just as the state is the presence of the universal within the particularist realm of civil society. As Friedrich Schiller puts it in his *Letters on the Aesthetic Education of Man* (1795):

> Every individual human being, one may say, carries within him, potentially and prescriptively, an ideal man, the archetype of a human being, and it is his life's task to be, through all his changing manifestations, in harmony with the unchanging unity of this ideal. This archetype, which is to be discerned more or less clearly in every individual, is represented by the State, the objective and, as it were, canonical form in which all the diversity of individual subjects strives to unite.[4]

In this tradition of thought, then, culture is neither dissociated from society nor wholly at one with it. If it is a critique of social life at one level, it is complicit with it at another. It has not yet set its face entirely against the actual, as it will as the English 'Culture and Society' lineage gradually unfurls. Indeed culture for Schiller is the very mechanism of what will later be called 'hegemony', moulding human subjects to the needs of a new kind of polity, remodelling them from the ground up into the docile, moderate, high-minded, peace-loving, uncontentious, disinterested agents of that political order. But to do this, culture must also act as a kind of immanent critique or deconstruction, occupying an unregenerate society from within to break down its resistance to the motions of the spirit. Later in the modern age, culture will become either Olympian wisdom or ideological weapon, a secluded form of social critique or a process locked all too deeply into the status quo. Here, at an earlier, more buoyant moment of that history, it is still possible to see culture as at once an ideal criticism and a real social force.

Raymond Williams has traced something of the complex history of the word 'culture', distinguishing three major modern senses of the word.[5] From its etymological roots in rural labour, the word comes first to mean something like 'civility', and then in the eighteenth century becomes more or less synonymous with 'civilization', in the sense of a general process of intellectual, spiritual and material progress. As an idea, civilization significantly equates manners and morals: to be civilized includes not spitting on the carpet as well as not decapitating one's prisoners of war. The very word implies a dubious correlation between mannerly conduct and ethical behaviour, which in England can also be found in the word 'gentleman'. As a synonym of 'civilization', 'culture' belonged to the general spirit of Enlightenment, with its cult of secular, progressive self-development. Civilization was largely a French notion – then as now, the French were thought to have a monopoly on being civilized – and named both the gradual process of social refinement and the utopian *telos* towards which it was unfolding. But whereas the French 'civilization' typically included political, economic and technical life, the German 'culture' had a more narrowly religious, artistic and intellectual reference. It could also mean the intellectual refinement of a group or individual, rather than of society as a whole. 'Civilization' played down national differences, whereas 'culture' highlighted them. The tension between 'culture' and 'civilization' had much to do with the rivalry between Germany and France.[6]

Three things then happen to the notion around the turn of the nineteenth century. For one thing, it begins to veer from being a synonym of 'civilization' towards being its antonym. This is a rare enough semantic swerve, and one which captures a momentous historical one. Like 'culture', 'civilization' is part-descriptive, part-normative: it can either neutrally designate a form of life ('Inca civilization'), or implicitly commend a life-form for its humanity, enlightenment and refinement. The adjectival form 'civilized' does this most obviously today. If civilization means the arts, urban living, civic politics, complex technologies and the like, and if this is considered an advance upon what went before, then 'civilization' is inseparably descriptive and normative. It means life as we know it, but also suggests that it is superior to barbarism. And if civilization is not only a stage of development in itself, but one which is constantly evolving within itself, then the word once more unifies fact and value. Any existing state of affairs implies a value-judgement, since it must logically be an improvement on what went before. Whatever is is not only right, but a great deal better than what was.

The trouble begins when the descriptive and normative aspects of the word 'civilization' start to fly apart. The term really belongs to the lexicon of a pre-industrial European middle class, redolent as it is of manners, refinement, *politesse*, an elegant ease of intercourse. It is thus both personal and social: cultivation is a matter of the harmonious, all-round development of the personality, but nobody can do this in isolation. Indeed it is the dawning recognition that they cannot which helps to shift culture from its individual to its social meaning. Culture requires certain social conditions; and since these conditions may involve the state, it can have a political dimension too. Cultivation goes hand in hand with commerce, since it is commerce which breaks down rural churlishness, brings men into complex relationship and thus polishes their rough edges. But the industrial-capitalist inheritors of this sanguine age would have rather more difficulty in persuading themselves that civilization as fact was at one with civilization as value. It is a fact of early industrial-capitalist civilization that young chimney sweeps tended to develop cancer of the scrotum, but it is hard to see it as a cultural achievement on a level with the Waverley novels or Rheims cathedral.

Meanwhile, by the end of the nineteenth century, 'civilization' had also acquired an inescapably imperialist echo, which was enough to discredit it in the eyes of some liberals. Another word was accordingly needed to denote how social life should be rather than how it was, and the Germans borrowed the French *culture* for the purpose. *Kultur* or Culture thus became the name of the Romantic, pre-Marxist critique of early industrial capitalism. Whereas civilization is a sociable term, a matter of genial wit and agreeable manners, culture is an altogether more portentous affair, spiritual, critical and high-minded rather than cheerfully at ease with the world. If the former is formulaically French, the latter is stereotypically German.

The more actual civilization appears predatory and debased, the more the idea of culture is forced into a critical attitude. *Kulturkritik* is at war with civilization rather than at one with it. If culture was once seen as allied with commerce, the two are now increasingly at odds. As Raymond Williams puts it, 'A word which had indicated a process of training within a more assured society became in the nineteenth century the focus of a deeply significant response to a society in the throes of a radical and painful change'.[7] One reason for the emergence of 'culture', then, is the fact that 'civilization' was beginning to ring less and less plausible as a value-term. So it is that the turn of the nineteenth century witnesses a growing *Kulturpessimismus*, of which perhaps the major document is Oswald Spengler's *Decline of the West*, but which finds its minor English resonance in F.R. Leavis's significantly entitled *Mass Civilisation and Minority Culture*. The copula of the title marks, needless to say, a glaring contrast.

If culture is to be an effective critique, however, it must retain its social dimension. It cannot simply lapse back into its earlier sense of individual cultivation. Coleridge's celebrated antithesis in *On the Constitution of Church and State* – 'The permanent distinction and the occasional contrast between cultivation and civilisation' – foreshadows much of the destiny of the word over the decades which were to follow. Born at the heart of the Enlightenment, the concept of culture now struck with Oedipal ferocity against its progenitors. Civilization was abstract, alienated, fragmented, mechanistic, utilitarian, in thrall to a crass faith in material progress; culture was holistic, organic, sensuous, autotelic, recollective. The conflict between culture and civilization thus belonged to a full-blown quarrel between tradition and modernity. But it was also to some extent a phoney war. The opposite of culture, for Matthew Arnold and his disciples, was an anarchy which was engendered by civilization itself. A grossly materialist society would breed its raw, resentful wreckers. But in refining these rebels, culture would find itself riding to the rescue of the very civilization for which it felt such disdain. Though the political wires between the two concepts were thus notoriously crossed, civilization was on the whole bourgeois, while culture was both patrician and populist. Like Lord Byron, it represented in the main a radical brand of aristocratism, with a heartfelt sympathy for the *Volk* and a supercilious distaste for the *Burgher.*

This *volkisch* turn of the concept is the second strand of development Williams traces. From the German Idealists onwards, culture comes to assume something of its modern meaning of a distinctive way of life. For Herder, this is a conscious assault on the universalism of the Enlightenment. Culture, he insists, means not some grand, unilinear narrative of universal humanity, but a diversity of specific life-forms, each with its own peculiar laws of evolution. In fact, as Robert Young points out, the Enlightenment was by no means uniformly opposed to this view. It could be open to non-European cultures in ways which perilously relativized its own values, and some of its thinkers prefigured the later idealizing of the 'primitive' as a critique of the West.[8] But Herder explicitly links the struggle between the two senses of the word 'culture' to a conflict between Europe and its colonial Others. He is out to oppose the Eurocentrism of culture-as-universal-civilization with the claims of those 'of all the quarters of the globe' who have not lived and perished for the dubious honour of having their posterity made happy by a speciously superior European culture.[9]

'What one nation holds indispensable to the circle of its thoughts', Herder writes, 'has never entered into the mind of a second, and by a third has been deemed injurious'.[10] The origin of the idea of culture as a distinctive way of life, then, is closely bound up with a Romantic anti-colonialist penchant for suppressed 'exotic' societies. The exoticism will resurface in the twentieth century in the primitivist features of modernism, a primitivism which goes hand-in-hand with the growth of modern cultural anthropology. It will crop up rather later, this time in postmodern guise, in a romanticizing of popular culture, which now plays the expressive, spontaneous, quasi-utopian role which 'primitive' cultures had played previously.[11]

In a gesture prefigurative of postmodernism, itself *inter alia* a vein of late Romantic thought, Herder proposes to pluralize the term 'culture', speaking as he does of the cultures of different nations and periods, as well as of distinct social and economic cultures within the nation itself. It is this sense of the word which will tentatively take root around the mid-nineteenth century, but which will not establish itself decisively until the beginning of the twentieth. Though the words 'civilization' and 'culture' go on being used interchangeably, not least by anthropologists, culture is now also almost the opposite of civility. It is tribal rather than cosmopolitan, a reality lived on the pulses at a level far deeper than the mind, and thus closed to rational criticism. Ironically, it is now a way of describing the life-forms of 'savages' rather than a term for the civilized.[12] In a curious reversal, savages are cultured but the civilized are not. But if 'culture' can describe a 'primitive' social order, it can also provide a way of idealizing one's own. For the radical Romantics, 'organic' culture could furnish a critique of actual society; for a thinker like Edmund Burke, it could provide a metaphor for actual society, and so shield it from such criticism. The unity some could find only in pre-modern communities could also be claimed of imperial Britain. Modern states could thus plunder pre-modern ones for ideological purposes as well as for economic ones. Culture is in this sense 'a word strictly improper, divided against itself . . . both synonymous with the mainstream of Western civilisation and antithetical to it'.[13] As a free play of disinterested thought, it can undermine selfish social interests; but since it undermines them in the name of the social whole, it reinforces the very social order it takes to task.

Culture as organic, like culture as civility, hovers indecisively between fact and value. In one sense, it does no more than designate a traditional form of life, whether of Berbers or barbers. But since community, tradition, rootedness and solidarity are notions we are supposed to approve of, at least until postmodernism happened along, there might be thought to be something affirmative in the sheer existence of such a life-form. Or, better, in the sheer fact of a plurality of such forms. It is this fusion of descriptive and normative, retained from both 'civilization' and the universalist sense of 'culture', which will rear its head in our own time in the guise of cultural relativism. Such 'postmodern' relativism derives, ironically, from just such ambiguities in the epoch of modernity itself. For the Romantics, there is something intrinsically precious about a whole way of life, not least if 'civilization' is busy disrupting it. Such 'wholeness' is no doubt a myth: anthropologists have taught us how 'the most heterogeneous habits, thoughts and actions may lie side by side'[14] in the most apparently 'primitive' of cultures, but the more rhapsodically minded have been conveniently deaf to this caveat. Whereas culture as civilization is rigorously discriminating, culture as way of life is not. What is good is whatever springs authentically from the people, whoever they may be. The case works rather better if you are thinking of, say, people like the Navajo rather than people like the Alabama Mothers for Moral Purity, but this was a distinction which was rapidly lost. Culture as civilization had borrowed its distinctions between high and low from early anthropology, for which some cultures were plainly superior to others; but as the debates unfolded, the anthropological sense of the word became more descriptive than evaluative. Simply being a culture of some kind was a value in itself; but it would no more make sense to elevate one such culture over another than to claim that the grammar of Catalan was superior to that of Arabic.

For the postmodernist, by contrast, whole ways of life are to be celebrated when they are those of dissident or minority groups, but to be castigated when they are those of majorities. Postmodern 'identity politics' thus include lesbianism but not nationalism, which for earlier Romantic radicals, as opposed to later postmodern ones, would be a wholly illogical move. The former camp, living through an era of political revolution, were protected from the absurdity of believing that majority movements or consensuses are invariably benighted. The latter camp, flourishing at a later, less euphoric phase of the same history, has abandoned a belief in radical mass movements, having precious few of them to remember. As a theory, postmodernism comes after the great mid-twentieth-century national liberation movements, and is either literally or metaphorically too young to recollect such seismic political upheavals. Indeed the very term 'post-colonialism' means a concern with 'Third World' societies which have already lived through their anti-colonial struggles, and which are thus unlikely to prove an embarrassment to those Western theorists who are fond of the underdog but distinctly more sceptical about such concepts as political revolution. It is also, perhaps, rather easier to feel solidarity with 'Third World' nations which are not currently in the business of killing one's compatriots.

To pluralize the concept of culture is not easily compatible with retaining its positive charge. It is simple enough to feel enthusiastic about culture as humanistic self-development, or even about, say, Bolivian culture, since any such complex formation is bound to include a good many benign features. But once one begins, in a spirit of generous pluralism, to break down the idea of culture to cover, say, 'police canteen culture', 'sexual-psychopath culture' or 'Mafia culture', then it is less evident that these are cultural forms to be approved simply because they are cultural forms. Or, indeed, simply because they are part of a rich diversity of such forms. Historically speaking, there has been a rich diversity of cultures of torture, but even devout pluralists would be loath to affirm this as one more instance of the colourful tapestry of human experience. Those who regard plurality as a value in itself are pure formalists, and have obviously not noticed the astonishingly imaginative variety of forms which, say, racism can assume. In any case, as with much postmodern thought, pluralism is here oddly crossed with self-identity. Rather than dissolving discrete identities, it multiplies them. Pluralism presupposes identity, rather as hybridization presupposes purity. Strictly speaking, one can only hybridize a culture which is pure; but as Edward Said suggests, 'all cultures are involved in one another; none is single and pure, all are hybrid, heterogeneous, extraordinarily differentiated, and unmonolithic'.[15] One needs to recall, too, that no human culture is more heterogeneous than capitalism.

If the first important variant in the word 'culture' is anti-capitalist critique, and the second a narrowing-cum-pluralizing of the notion to a whole way of life, the third is its gradual specialization to the arts. Even here the word can be shrunk or expanded, since culture in this sense can include intellectual activity in general (science, philosophy, scholarship and the like), or be slimmed down even further to allegedly more 'imaginative' pursuits such as music, painting and literature. 'Cultured' people are people who have culture in this sense. This sense of the word, too, signals a dramatic historical development. It suggests, for one thing, that science, philosophy, politics and economics can no longer be regarded as creative or imaginative. It also suggests – to put the case at its bleakest – that 'civilized' values are now to be found only in fantasy. And this is clearly a caustic comment on social reality. If creativity could now be found in art, was this because it could be found nowhere else? Once culture comes to mean learning and the arts, activities confined to a tiny proportion of men and women, the idea is at once intensified and impoverished.

The story of what this will do to the arts themselves, as they find themselves accorded a momentous social significance which they are really too fragile and delicate to sustain, crumbling from the inside as they are forced to stand in for God or happiness or political justice, belongs to the narrative of modernism. It is postmodernism which seeks to relieve the arts of this oppressive burden of anxiety, urging them to forget all such portentous dreams of depth, and thus liberating them into a fairly trifling sort of freedom. Long before then, however, Romanticism had tried to square the circle between finding in aesthetic culture an alternative to politics, and finding in it the very paradigm of a transformed political order. This was not quite as hard as it seems, since if the whole point of art was its pointlessness, then the most flamboyant aestheticist was also in a sense the most dedicated revolutionary, pledged to an idea of value as self-validating which was the very reverse of capitalist utility. Art could now model the good life not by representing it but simply by being itself, by what it showed rather than by what it said, offering the scandal of its own pointlessly self-delighting existence as a silent critique of exchange-value and instrumental rationality. But this elevation of art in the service of humanity was inevitably self-undoing, as it lent the Romantic artist a transcendent status at odds with his or her political significance, and as, in the perilous trap of all utopia, the image of the good life came gradually to stand in for its actual unavailability.

Culture was self-undoing in another sense too. What made it critical of industrial capitalism was its affirmation of wholeness, symmetry, the all-round development of human capacities. From Schiller to Ruskin, this wholeness is set against the lop-sided effects of a division of labour which stunts and narrows human powers. Marxism, too, has some of its sources in this Romantic-humanist tradition. But if culture is a free, self-delighting play of spirit in which all human capacities can be disinterestedly cherished, then it is also an idea which sets its face firmly against partisanship. To be committed is to be uncultivated. Matthew Arnold may have believed in culture as social improvement, but he also refused to take sides over the slavery question in the American civil war. Culture is thus an antidote to politics, tempering that fanatical tunnel vision in its appeal to equipoise, to keeping the mind serenely untainted by whatever is tendentious, unbalanced, sectarian. Indeed for all postmodernism's dislike of liberal humanism, there is more than a hint of that vision in its own pluralist unease with hard-and-fast positions, its mistaking of the determinate for the dogmatic. Culture, then, may be a critique of capitalism, but it is just as much a critique of the commitments which oppose it. For its many-sided ideal to be realized, a strenuously one-sided politics would be necessary; but the means would then run disastrously counter to the end. Culture requires of those clamouring for justice that they look beyond their own partial interests to the whole – which is to say, to their rulers' interests as well as their own. It can then make nothing of the fact that these interests may be mutually contradictory. For culture to become associated with justice for minority groups, as it has been in our own time, is thus a decisively new development.

In this refusal of partisanship, culture appears a politically neutral notion. But it is precisely in this formal commitment to many-sidedness that it is most clamorously partisan. Culture is indifferent to which human faculties should be realized, and so would seem genuinely disinterested at the level of content. It insists only that these faculties must be realized harmoniously, each judiciously counterbalancing the other, and thus insinuates a politics at the level of form. We are asked to believe that unity is inherently preferable to conflict, or symmetry to one-sidedness. We are also asked to believe, even more implausibly, that this is not itself a political position. Similarly, since these powers are to be realized purely for their own sake, culture can hardly stand accused of political instrumentality. But there is, in fact, a politics implicit precisely in this non-utility – either the patrician politics of those who have the leisure and liberty to cast utility disdainfully to one side, or the utopian politics of those who wish to see a society beyond exchange-value.

It is not, in fact, just culture, but a particular selection of cultural values, which is in question here. To be civilized or cultivated is to be blessed with refined feelings, well-tempered passions, agreeable manners and an open mind. It is to behave reasonably and moderately, with an innate sensitivity to others' interests, to exercise self-discipline, and to be prepared to sacrifice one's own selfish interests to the good of the whole. However splendid some of these prescriptions may be, they are certainly not politically innocent. On the contrary, the cultivated individual sounds suspiciously like a mildly conservative liberal. It is as though BBC newscasters set the paradigm for humanity at large. This civilized individual certainly does not sound like a political revolutionary, even though revolution is part of civilization too. The word 'reasonable' here means something like 'open to persuasion' or 'willing to compromise', as though all passionate conviction was *ipso facto* irrational. Culture is on the side of sentiment rather than passion, which is to say on the side of the mannered middle classes rather than the irate masses. Given the importance of equipoise, it is hard to see why one would not be required to counterbalance an objection to racism with its opposite. To be unequivocally opposed to racism would seem distinctly non-pluralist. Since moderation is always a virtue, a mild distaste for child prostitution would seem more appropriate than a vehement opposition to it. And since action would seem to imply a fairly definitive set of choices, this version of culture is inevitably more contemplative than *engagé*.

Such, at least, would seem true of Friedrich Schiller's notion of the aesthetic, which he presents to us as a 'negative state of complete absence of determination'.[16] In the aesthetic condition, 'man is Nought, if we are thinking of any particular result rather than of the totality of his powers'[17]; we are suspended instead in a state of perpetual possibility, a kind of nirvanic negation of all determinacy. Culture, or the aesthetic, is without bias to any specific social interest, but precisely on that account is a general activating capacity. It is not so much opposed to action, as the creative source of any action whatsoever. Culture, 'because it takes under its protection no single one of man's faculties to the exclusion of the others . . . favours each and all of them without distinction; and it favours no single one more than another for the simple reason that it is the ground of possibility of them all'.[18] Unable, as it were, to say one thing without saying anything, culture says nothing whatsoever, so boundlessly eloquent as to be speechless. In cultivating every possibility to its limit, it risks leaving us muscle-bound and immobilized. Such is the paralytic effect of Romantic irony. When we do come to act, we close off this free play with the sordidly specific; but at least we do so in the awareness of other possibilities, and allow that unbounded sense of creative potential to inform whatever it is we do.

For Schiller, then, culture would seem at once the source of action and the negation of it. There is a tension between what makes our practice creative, and the very earth-bound fact of practice itself. For Matthew Arnold, rather similarly, culture is at once an ideal of absolute perfection and the imperfect historical process which labours to that end. In both cases, there would seem to be some constitutive gap between culture and its fleshly incarnation, as the many-sidedness of the aesthetic inspires us to actions which contradict it in their very determinateness.

If the word 'culture' is an historical and philosophical text, it is also the site of a political conflict. As Raymond Williams puts it: 'The complex of senses (within the term) indicates a complex argument about the relations between general human development and a particular way of life, and between both and the works and practices of art and intelligence'.[19] This, in fact, is the narrative traced in Williams's

Culture and Society 1780–1950, which charts the indigenous English version of European *Kulturphilosophie*. One might see this current of thought as struggling to connect various meanings of culture which are gradually floating apart: culture (in the sense of the arts) defines a quality of fine living (culture as civility) which it is the task of political change to realize in culture (in the sense of social life) as a whole. The aesthetic and anthropological are thus reunited. From Coleridge to F.R. Leavis, the broader, socially responsible sense of culture is kept firmly in play, but can only be defined by a more specialized sense of the term (culture as the arts) which threatens constantly to substitute for it. In a stalled dialectic of these two senses of culture, Arnold and Ruskin recognize that without social change, the arts and 'fine living' themselves are in deadly danger; yet they also believe that the arts are among the forlornly few instruments of such transformation. In England, it is not until William Morris, who harnesses this *Kulturphilosophie* to an actual political force – the working-class movement – that this vicious semantic circle can be broken.

The Williams of *Keywords* is perhaps not alert enough to the inner logic of the changes he records. What is it that connects culture as utopian critique, culture as way of life and culture as artistic creation? The answer is surely a negative one: all three are in different ways reactions to the failure of culture as actual civilization – as the grand narrative of human self-development. If this becomes a hard story to credit as industrial capitalism unfolds, a tall tale inherited from a somewhat more sanguine past, then the idea of culture is faced with some unpalatable alternatives. It can retain its global reach and social relevance, but recoil from the dismal present to become a poignantly endangered image of a desirable future. Another such image, unexpectedly enough, is the ancient past, which resembles an emancipated future in the sheer unignorable fact of its non-existence. This is culture as utopian critique, at once prodigiously creative and politically enervated, which is always in danger of disappearing into the very critical distance from *Realpolitik* it so devastatingly establishes.

Alternatively, culture can survive by abjuring all such abstraction and going concrete, becoming the culture of Bavaria or Microsoft or the Bushmen; but this risks lending it a much-needed specificity in proportion to its loss of normativity. For the Romantics, this sense of culture retains its normative force, since these forms of *Gemeinschaft* can be drawn on for a resourceful critique of industrial-capitalist *Gesellschaft*. Postmodern thought, by contrast, is far too allergic to nostalgia to take this sentimentalist path, forgetful that for a Walter Benjamin even nostalgia can be given a revolutionary meaning. What is valuable for postmodern theory is more the formal fact of the plurality of these cultures than their intrinsic content. In fact as far as their content goes there can really be nothing to choose between them, since the criteria of any such choice must themselves be culture-bound. The concept of culture thus gains in specificity what it loses in critical capacity, rather as the Constructivist rocking-chair is a more sociable art-form than the high modernist artwork, but only at the cost of its critical edge.

The third response to the crisis of culture as civilization, as we have seen, is to shrink the whole category to a handful of artistic works. Culture here means a body of artistic and intellectual work of agreed value, along with the institutions which produce, disseminate and regulate it. In this fairly recent meaning of the word, culture is both symptom and solution. If culture is an oasis of value, then it offers a solution of sorts. But if learning and the arts are the sole surviving enclaves of creativity, then we are most certainly in dire trouble. Under what social conditions does creativity become confined to music and poetry, while science, technology, politics, work and domesticity become drearily prosaic? One can ask of this notion of culture what Marx famously inquired of religion: For what grievous estrangement is such transcendence a poor compensation?

Yet this minority idea of culture, however much a symptom of historical crisis, is also a kind of solution. Like culture as way of life, it lends tone and texture to the Enlightenment abstraction of culture as civilization. In the most fertile currents of English literary criticism from Wordsworth to Orwell, it is the arts, not least the arts of ordinary language, which offer a sensitive index of the quality of social life as a whole. But if culture in this sense of the word has the sensuous immediacy of culture as way of life, it also inherits the normative bias of culture as civilization. The arts may reflect fine living, but they are also the measure of it. If they embody, they also evaluate. In this sense, they link the actual and the desirable in the manner of a radical politics.

The three distinct senses of culture are thus not easily separable. If culture as critique is to be more than idle fantasy, it must point to those practices in the present which prefigure something of the friendship and fulfilment for which it yearns. It finds these partly in artistic production, and partly in those marginal cultures which have not yet been wholly absorbed by the logic of utility. By roping in culture in these other senses, culture as critique tries to avoid the purely subjunctive mood of 'bad' utopia, which consists simply in a sort of wistful yearning, a 'wouldn't it be nice if' with no basis in the actual. The political equivalent of this is the infantile disorder known as ultraleftism, which negates the present in the name of some inconceivably alternative future. 'Good' utopia, by contrast, finds a bridge between present and future in those forces within the present which are potentially able to transform it. A desirable future must also be a feasible one. By linking itself to these other senses of culture, which at least have the virtue of actually existing, the more utopian brand of culture can thus become a form of immanent critique, judging the present to be lacking by measuring it against norms which it has generated itself. In this sense, too, culture can unite fact and value, as both an account of the actual and a foretaste of the desirable. If the actual contains that which contradicts it, then the term 'culture' is bound to face both ways. Deconstruction, which shows how a situation it is bound to violate its own logic in the very effort to adhere to it, is simply a more recent name for this traditional notion of immanent critique. For the radical Romantics, art, the imagination, folk culture or 'primitive' communities are signs of a creative energy which must be spread to political society as a whole. For Marxism, arriving in Romanticism's wake, it is a rather less exalted form of creative energy, that of the working class, which might transfigure the very social order of which it is the product.

Culture in this sense arises when civilization begins to seem self-contradictory. As civilized society unfolds, there comes a point where it forces upon some of its theorists a strikingly new kind of reflection, known as dialectical thought. This is, as it were, a response to a certain embarrassment. Dialectical thought arises because it is less and less possible to ignore the fact that civilization, in the very act of realizing some human potentials, also damagingly suppresses others. It is the internal relation between these two processes which breeds this new intellectual habit. You can rationalize this contradiction by confining the word 'civilization' to a value-term and contrasting it with present-day society. This, presumably, is what Gandhi had in mind when asked what he thought of British civilization: 'I think it would be a very good idea'. But one can also dub the suppressed capacities 'culture', and the repressive ones 'civilization'. The virtue of this move is that culture can act as a critique of the present while being based solidly within it. It is neither the mere other of society, nor (as with 'civilization') identical with it, but moves both with and against the grain of historical progress. Culture is not some vague fantasy of fulfilment, but a set of potentials bred by history and subversively at work within it.

The trick is to know how to unlock these capacities, and Marx's answer will be socialism. For him, nothing in the socialist future can be authentic unless it somehow takes its cue from the capitalist present. But if it is a chastening thought that the positive and negative aspects of history are so closely linked, it is also an inspiring one. For the truth is that repression, exploitation and the like would not work unless there were reasonably autonomous, reflective, resourceful human beings to exploit or be exploited. There is no need to repress creative capacities which do not exist. These are scarcely the soundest reasons for rejoicing. It seems odd to foster faith in human beings on the grounds that they are capable of being exploited. Even so, it is true that those more benign cultural practices we know as nurture are implicit in the very existence of injustice. Only someone who has been cared for as an infant can be unjust, since otherwise he would not be around to abuse you. All cultures must include such practices as child-rearing, education, welfare, communication, mutual support, otherwise they would be unable to reproduce themselves, and thus unable among other things to engage in exploitative practices. Of course child-rearing can be sadistic, communication garbled and education brutally autocratic. But no culture can be entirely negative, since just to achieve its vicious ends it must foster capacities which always imply virtuous uses. Torture requires the sort of judgement, initiative and intelligence which can also be used to abolish it. In this sense, all cultures are self-contradictory. But this is grounds for hope as well as cynicism, since it means that they themselves breed the forces which might transform them. It is not a matter of parachuting in such forces from some metaphysical outer space.

There are other ways in which these three senses of culture interact. The idea of culture as an organic way of life belongs to 'high' culture quite as much as Berlioz does. As a concept, it is the product of cultivated intellectuals, and can represent the primordial other which might revitalize their own degenerate societies. Whenever one hears admiring talk of the savage, one can be sure that one is in the presence of sophisticates. Indeed it took a sophisticate, Sigmund Freud, to reveal what incestuous desires may lurk within our dreams of sensuous wholeness, our hankering for a body which is warmly palpable yet eternally elusive. Culture, which is at once a concrete reality and a cloudy vision of perfection, captures something of this duality. Modernist art turns to these primeval notions in order to survive a philistine modernity, and mythology provides a pivot between the two. The overbred and the underdeveloped forge strange alliances.

But the two notions of culture are related in other ways too. Culture as the arts may be the harbinger of a new social existence, but the case is curiously circular, since without such social change the arts themselves are in jeopardy. The artistic imagination, so the argument runs, can flourish only in an organic social order, and will not take root in the shallow soil of modernity. Individual cultivation now depends more and more on culture in its social sense. So it is that Henry James and T.S. Eliot abandon the 'inorganic' society of their native United States for a more mannered, devious, richly sedimented Europe. If the United States stands for civilization, a thoroughly secular notion, Europe symbolizes culture, a quasi-religious one. Art is fatally compromised by a society which enthuses over it only in the auction room, and whose abstract logic strips the world of sensuousness. It is also tainted by a social order for which truth has no utility, and value means what will sell. Just for the arts to survive, then, it might be necessary to become a political reactionary or revolutionary, wind back the clock *à la* Ruskin to the corporate order of feudal Gothic or wind it forward with William Morris to a socialism which has outlived the commodity form.

It is just as easy, however, to see these two senses of culture as locked in contention. Is not overbredness the enemy of action? Might not the cloistered, nuanced, myriad-minded sensitivity which the arts bring with them unfit us for broader, less ambivalent commitments? One would not generally assign the chair of the sanitation committee to a poet. Does not the focused intensity which the fine arts demand disable us for such humdrum affairs, even if it is on socially conscious artworks that we bend our attention? As for the more *gemeinschaftlich* sense of culture, it is not hard to see how this involves a transference to society of the values linked with culture as art. Culture as way of life is an aestheticized version of society, finding in it the unity, sensuous immediacy and freedom from conflict which we associate with the aesthetic artefact. The word 'culture', which is supposed to designate a kind of society, is in fact a normative way of imagining that society. It can also be a way of imagining one's own social conditions on the model of other people's, either in the past, the bush, or the political future.

Though culture is a popular word with postmodernism, its most important sources remain pre-modern. As an idea, culture begins to matter at four points of historical crisis: when it becomes the only apparent alternative to a degraded society; when it seems that without deep-seated social change, culture in the sense of the arts and fine living will no longer even be possible; when it provides the terms in which a group or people seeks its political emancipation; and when an imperialist power is forced to come to terms with the way of life of those it subjugates. Of these, it is probably the latter pair which have put the idea most decisively on the twentieth-century agenda. We owe our modern notion of culture in large part to nationalism and colonialism, along with the growth of an anthropology in the service of imperial power. At roughly the same historical point, the emergence of 'mass' culture in the West lent the concept an added urgency. It is with Romantic nationalists like Herder and Fichte that the idea of a distinct ethnic culture, with political rights simply by virtue of this ethnic peculiarity, first springs up;[20] and culture is vital to nationalism in the way that it is not, or not so much, to, say, class struggle, civil rights or famine relief. On one view, nationalism is what adapts primordial bonds to modern complexities. As the pre-modern nation gives way to the modern nation-state, the structure of traditional roles can no longer hold society together, and it is culture, in the sense of a common language, inheritance, educational system, shared values and the like, which steps in as the principle of social unity.[21] Culture, in other words, comes to prominence intellectually when it becomes a force to be reckoned with politically.

It is with the unfolding of nineteenth-century colonialism that the anthropological meaning of culture as a unique way of life first starts to take grip. And the way of life in question is usually that of the 'uncivilized'. As we have seen already, culture as civility is the opposite of barbarism, but culture as a way of life can be identical with it. Herder, so Geoffrey Hartman considers, is the first to use the word culture 'in the modern sense of an *identity culture*: a sociable, populist, and traditionary way of life, characterised by a quality that pervades everything and makes a person feel rooted or at home'.[22] Culture, in short, is other people.[23] As Fredric Jameson has argued, culture is always 'an idea of the Other (even when I reassume it for myself)'.[24] It is unlikely that the Victorians thought of themselves as a 'culture'; this would not only have meant seeing themselves in the round, but seeing themselves as just one possible life-form among many. To define one's life-world as a culture is to risk relativizing it. One's own way of life is simply human; it is other people who are ethnic, idiosyncratic, culturally peculiar. In a similar way, one's own views are reasonable, while other people's are extremist.

If the science of anthropology marks the point where the West begins to convert other societies into legitimate objects of study, the real sign of political crisis is when it feels the need to do this to itself. For there are savages within Western society too, enigmatic, half-intelligible creatures ruled by ferocious passions and given to mutinous behaviour; and these too will need to become objects of disciplined knowledge. Positivism, the first self-consciously 'scientific' school of sociology, discloses the evolutionary laws by which industrial society is becoming inexorably more corporate, laws which an unruly proletariat needs to recognize as no more violable than the forces which stir the waves. Somewhat later, it will be part of the task of anthropology to conspire in 'the massive perceptual illusion through which a nascent imperialism brought "savages" into being, freezing them conceptually in their sub-human otherness even as it disrupted their social formations and liquidated them physically'.[25]

The Romantic version of culture thus evolved over time into a 'scientific' one. But there were key affinities even so. The former's idealizing of the 'folk', of vital sub-cultures buried deep within its own society, could be transferred easily enough to those primitive types who lived abroad rather than at home. Both folk and primitives are residues of the past within the present, quaintly archaic beings who crop up like so many time-warps within the contemporary. Romantic organicism could thus be recast as anthropological functionalism, grasping such 'primitive' cultures as coherent and non-contradictory. The word 'whole' in the phrase 'a whole way of life' floats ambiguously between fact and value, meaning a form of life you can grasp in the round because you are standing outside it, but also one with an integrity of being lacking to your own. Culture thus places your own agnostic, atomistic way of life under judgement, but quite literally from a long way off.

Moreover, the idea of culture, all the way from its etymological origins in the tending of natural growth, had always been a way of decentring consciousness. If it meant in its narrower usage the finest, most exquisitely conscious products of human history, its more general meaning signalled exactly the opposite. With its resonance of organic process and stealthy evolution, culture was a quasi-determinist concept, meaning those features of social life – custom, kinship, language, ritual, mythology – which choose us far more than we choose them. Ironically, then, the idea of culture cut both above and below ordinary social life, at once incomparably more conscious and considerably less calculable. 'Civilization', by contrast, has a ring of agency and awareness about it, an aura of rational projection and urban planning, as a collective project by which cities are wrested from swamps and cathedrals raised to the skies. Part of the scandal of Marxism had been to treat civilization as though it were culture – to write, in short, the history of humanity's political unconscious, of those social processes which, as Marx put it, go on 'behind the backs' of the agents concerned. As with Freud a little later, a finely civilized consciousness is dislodged to reveal the hidden forces which put it in place. As one reviewer of *Capital* commented to its author's approval: 'If in the history of civilisation, the conscious elements play a part so subordinate, then it is self-evident that a critical enquiry whose subject-matter is civilisation, can, less than anything else, have for its basis any form of, or any result of, consciousness'.[26]

Culture, then, is the unconscious *verso* of the *recto* of civilized life, the taken-for-granted beliefs and predilections which must be dimly present for us to be able to act at all. It is what comes naturally, bred in the bone rather than conceived by the brain. It is not surprising, then, that the concept should have found such a hospitable place in the study of 'primitive' societies, which in the eyes of the anthropologist allowed their myths, rituals, kinship systems and ancestral traditions to do their thinking for them. They were a kind of South Sea island version of English common law and the House of Lords, living in a Burkeian utopia in which instinct, custom, piety and ancestral law worked all by themselves, without the meddling intervention of analytical reason. The 'savage mind' thus had a particular importance for cultural modernism, which from T.S. Eliot's fertility cults to Stravinsky's rites of spring could find in it a shadowy critique of Enlightenment rationality.

One could even have one's theoretical cake and eat it, finding in these 'primitive' cultures both a critique of such rationality and a confirmation of it. If their supposedly concrete, sensuous habits of thought offered a rebuke to the desiccated reason of the West, the unconscious codes which governed that thought had all the exacting rigour of algebra or linguistics. So it was that the structural anthropology of Claude Lévi-Strauss could present such 'primitives' as both consolingly similar to and exotically different from ourselves. If they thought in terms of earth and moon, they did so with all the elegant complexity of nuclear physics.[27] Tradition and modernity could thus be agreeably harmonized, a project which structuralism had inherited, unfinished, from high modernism. The most avant-garde mentality thus turned full circle to meet up with the most archaic; indeed for some Romantic thinkers it was only in this way that a dissolute Western culture could be regenerated. Having reached a point of complex decadence, civilization could refresh itself only at the fountain of culture, looking backward in order to move forward. Modernism accordingly put time into reverse gear, finding in the past an image of the future.

Structuralism was not the only branch of literary theory which could trace some of its origins back to imperialism. Hermeneutics, behind which lurks an anxious query as to whether the other is intelligible at all, is hardly irrelevant to the project, and neither is psychoanalysis, which unearths an atavistic subtext at the very roots of human consciousness. Mythological or archetypal criticism does something of the same, while post-structuralism, one of whose leading exponents hails from a former French colony, calls into question what it sees as a profoundly Eurocentric metaphysics. As for postmodern theory, nothing could be less to its taste than the idea of a stable, pre-modern, tightly unified culture, at the very thought of which it reaches for its hybridity and open-endedness. But the post- and pre-modern are more akin than this would suggest. What they share in common is the high, sometimes extravagant respect they accord to culture as such. In fact one might claim that culture is a pre-modern and postmodern rather than modern idea; if it flourishes in the era of modernity, it is largely as a trace of the past or an anticipation of the future.

What links pre-modern and postmodern orders is that for both, though for quite different reasons, culture is a dominant level of social life. If it bulks so large in traditional societies, it is because it is less a 'level' at all than a pervasive medium within which other kinds of activity go on. Politics, sexuality and economic production are still caught up to some extent in a symbolic order of meaning. As the anthropologist Marshall Sahlins observes, in a smack at the Marxist base/superstructure model, 'In the tribal cultures, economy, polity, ritual, and ideology do not appear as distinct "systems"'.[28] In the postmodern world, culture and social life are once again closely allied, but now in the shape of the aesthetics of the commodity, the spectacularization of politics, the consumerism of life-style, the centrality of the image, and the final integration of culture into commodity production in general. Aesthetics, which began life as a term for everyday perceptual experience and only later became specialized to art, had now come full circle and rejoined its mundane origin, just as two senses of culture – the arts and the common life – had now been conflated in style, fashion, advertising, media and the like.

What happens in between is modernity, for which culture is not the most vital of concepts. Indeed it is hard for us to think ourselves back to a time when all of our own most fashionable buzz-words – *bodiliness, difference, locality, imagination, cultural identity* – were seen as the obstacles to an emancipatory politics, rather than its terms of reference. Culture for the Enlightenment meant, roughly speaking, those regressive attachments which prevented us from entering upon our citizenship of the world. It signified our sentiment for place, nostalgia for tradition, preference for tribe, reverence for hierarchy. Difference was largely a reactionary doctrine which denied the equality to which all men and women were entitled. An assault on Reason in the name of intuition or the wisdom of the body was a charter for mindless prejudice. Imagination was a sickness of the mind which prevented us from seeing the world as it was, and so of acting to transform it. And to deny Nature in the name of Culture was almost certainly to end up on the wrong side of the barricades.

Culture, to be sure, still had its place; but as the modern age unfolded, that place was either oppositional or supplementary. Either culture became a rather toothless form of political critique, or it was the protected area into which one could siphon off all of those potentially disruptive energies, spiritual, artistic or erotic, for which modernity could make less and less provision. This area, like most officially sacred spaces, was both venerated and ignored, centred and sidelined. Culture was no longer a description of what one was, but of what one might be or used to be. It was less a name for your own group than for your bohemian dissenters, or, as the nineteenth century drew on, for less sophisticated peoples living a long way off. For culture no longer to describe social existence as it is speaks eloquently of a certain kind of society. As Andrew Milner points out, 'it is only in modern industrial democracies that "culture" and "society" become excluded from both politics and economics . . . modern society is understood as distinctively and unusually asocial, its economic and political life characteristically "normless" and "value-free", in short, uncultured'.[29] Our very notion of culture thus rests on a peculiarly modern alienation of the social from the economic, meaning from material life. Only in a society whose everyday existence seems drained of value could 'culture' come to exclude material reproduction; yet only in this way could the concept become a critique of that life. As Raymond Williams comments, culture emerges as a notion from 'the recognition of the practical separation of certain moral and intellectual activities from the driven impetus of a new kind of society'. This notion then becomes 'a court of human appeal, to be set over the processes of practical social judgement . . . as a mitigating and rallying alternative'.[30] Culture is thus symptomatic of a division which it offers to overcome. As the sceptic remarked of psychoanalysis, it is itself the illness to which it proposes a cure.

2

Culture in Crisis

It is hard to resist the conclusion that the word 'culture' is both too broad and too narrow to be greatly useful. Its anthropological meaning covers everything from hairstyles and drinking habits to how to address your husband's second cousin, while the aesthetic sense of the word includes Igor Stravinsky but not science fiction. Science fiction belongs to 'mass' or popular culture, a category which floats ambiguously between the anthropological and the aesthetic. Conversely, one can see the aesthetic meaning as too nebulous and the anthropological one as too cramping. The Arnoldian sense of culture as perfection, sweetness and light, the best that has been thought and said, seeing the object as it really is and so on, is embarrassingly imprecise, whereas if culture just signifies the way of life of Turkish physiotherapists then it seems uncomfortably specific. It is the contention of this book that we are trapped at the moment between disablingly wide and discomfortingly rigid notions of culture, and that our most urgent need in the area is to move beyond both. Margaret Archer observes that the concept of culture has displayed 'the weakest analytical development of any key concept in sociology and it has played the most wildly vacillating role within sociological theory'.[1] A case in point is Edward Sapir's assertion that 'culture is defined in terms of forms of behaviour, and the content of culture is made up of these forms, of which there are countless numbers'.[2] It would be hard to come up with a more resplendently empty definition.

How much in any case does culture as way of life include? Can a way of life be too large and diverse to be spoken of as a culture, or too small? Raymond Williams sees the scope of a culture 'as usually proportionate to the area of a language rather than to the area of a class',[3] though this is surely doubtful: the English language spans a great many cultures, and postmodern culture covers a diverse span of languages. Australian culture, Andrew Milner suggests, consists of 'distinctively Australian ways of doing things: the beach and the barbecue, mateship and machismo, *Hungry Jack's*, the arbitration system and Australian rules football'.[4] But 'distinctive' here cannot mean 'peculiar', since machismo, alas, is not confined to Australia, and neither are beaches and barbecues. Milner's suggestive list mixes items which are peculiar to Australia with non-peculiar ones which bulk large in it. 'British culture' includes Warwick castle but not usually the manufacture of drainpipes, a ploughman's lunch but not a ploughman's wages. Despite the apparently all-inclusive sweep of the anthropological definition, some things are felt to be too mundane to be cultural, while others are felt to be too undistinctive. Since the British manufacture drainpipes in much the same way as the Japanese do, dressed in no fetching national costume and chanting no rousing traditional ballads in the process, drainpipe-making falls out of the category of culture as both too prosaic and too non-specific. Yet the study of Nuer or Tuareg culture might well include the tribe's economy. And if culture means whatever is humanly constructed rather than naturally given, then this ought logically to include industry as well as media, ways of making rubber ducks as well as ways of making love or making merry.

Perhaps practices like drainpipe manufacture fail to be cultural because they are not *signifying* practices, a semiotic definition of culture which was ephemerally popular in the 1970s. Clifford Geertz, for example, sees culture as the webs of signification in which humanity is suspended.[5] Raymond Williams writes of culture as 'the signifying system through which . . . a social order is communicated, reproduced, experienced and explored'.[6] Behind this definition lurks a structuralist sense of the *active* nature of signification, which fits with Williams's proto-post-Marxist insistence that culture is constitutive of other social processes, rather than merely reflecting or representing them. This sort of formulation has the advantage of being specific enough to mean something ('signifying'), but broad enough to be non-elitist. It could take in both Voltaire and vodka ads. But if car-making falls outside this definition, so does sport, which like any human practice involves signification, but is hardly in the same cultural category as Homeric epic and graffiti. Indeed Williams is keen to distinguish among different degrees of signification here, or rather among different ratios between signification and what he calls 'need'. All social systems involve signification, but there is a difference between literature and, say, coinage, where the signifying factor is 'dissolved' into the functional one, or between television and the telephone. Housing is a matter of need, but only becomes a signifying system when social distinctions begin to loom large within it. A sandwich snatched in haste differs in the same respect from a meal at the Ritz savoured at leisure. Hardly anyone dines at the Ritz just because they are hungry. All social systems, then, involve signification, but not all of them are signifying or 'cultural' systems. This is a valuable distinction, avoiding as it does both jealously exclusive and uselessly inclusive definitions of culture. But it is really a reworking of the traditional aesthetic/instrumental dichotomy, and is open to the kind of objection which this has customarily attracted.

Culture can be loosely summarized as the complex of values, customs, beliefs and practices which constitute the way of life of a specific group. It is 'that complex whole', as the anthropologist E.B. Tylor famously puts it in his *Primitive Culture*, 'which includes knowledge, belief, art, morals, law, custom, and any other capabilities and habits acquired by man as a member of society'.[7] But 'any other capabilities' is rather recklessly open-minded: the cultural and the social then become effectively identical. Culture is just everything which is not genetically transmissable. It is, as one sociologist puts it, the belief that human beings 'are what they are taught'.[8] Stuart Hall offers a similarly generous view of culture as the 'lived practices' or 'practical ideologies which enable a society, group or class to experience, define, interpret and make sense of its conditions of existence'.[9]

On another view, culture is the implicit knowledge of the world by which people negotiate appropriate ways of acting in specific contexts. Like Aristotle's *phronesis*, it is more know-how than know-why, a set of tacit understandings or practical guidelines as opposed to a theoretical mapping of reality. You can see culture rather more specifically as, in John Frow's words, 'the whole range of practices and representations through which a social group's reality (or realities) is constructed and maintained',[10] which would probably exclude the fishing industry but might exclude cricket too. Cricket can certainly be part of a society's self-image, but it is not exactly a representational practice in the sense that surrealist poetry or Orange marches are.

In a very early essay, Raymond Williams includes 'the idea of a standard of perfection' among the classical definitions of culture.[11] Later, in *Culture and Society 1780–1950*, he offers four distinct meanings of culture: as an individual habit of mind; as the state of intellectual development of a whole society; as the arts; and as the whole way of life of a group of people.[12] One might think the first of these too narrow and the last of them too wide; but Williams has a political motive for this final definition, since to restrict culture to the arts and intellectual life is to risk excluding the working class from the category. Once, however, you expand it to include institutions – trade unions and cooperatives, for example – you can justly argue that the working class has produced a rich, complex culture, though not one which is primarily artistic. On this definition, however, fire stations and public lavatories might also need to be included in the idea of culture, since they too are institutions – in which case culture becomes co-extensive with society and risks losing its conceptual cutting-edge. In one sense, the phrase 'cultural institution' is a tautology, since there are no non-cultural ones. You might argue, however, that trade unions are cultural institutions because they express collective meanings, whereas public lavatories do not. In *The Long Revolution*, Williams's definition of culture includes 'the organisation of production, the structure of the family, the structure of institutions which express or govern social relationships, the characteristic forms through which members of the society communicate'.[13] This is no doubt excessively generous, leaving almost nothing out.

Elsewhere in the same work, Williams proposes yet another definition of culture as a 'structure of feeling', a quasi-oxymoronic notion that captures the sense that culture is at once definite and impalpable. A structure of feeling 'is the particular living result of all the elements in the general organisation (of a society) . . . I would define the theory of culture as the study of relationships between elements in a whole way of life'.[14] 'Structure of feeling', with its bold yoking of the objective and the affective, is a way of trying to negotiate the doubleness of culture, as at once material reality and lived experience. Anyway, the complexity of the idea of culture is nowhere more graphically demonstrated than in the fact that its most eminent theorist in post-war Britain, Raymond Williams, defines it at various times to mean a standard of perfection, a habit of mind, the arts, general intellectual development, a whole way of life, a signifying system, a structure of feeling, the interrelation of elements in a way of life, and everything from economic production and the family to political institutions.

Alternatively, you can try to define culture functionally rather than substantively, as whatever is superfluous to a society's material requirements. On this theory, food is not cultural but sun-dried tomatoes are; labour is not cultural but wearing hob-nailed boots while engaged in it is. In most climates, wearing clothes is a matter of physical necessity, but what kind of clothes you wear is not. There is some point to this idea of culture as surplus, which is not far from Williams's ratio between signification and need; but the problem of distinguishing between what is and is not surplus is fairly daunting. People might well riot over tobacco or Taoism more readily than they would over more materially pressing matters. And once cultural production has become part of general commodity production, it is more than usually difficult to say where the realm of necessity ends and the kingdom of freedom begins. Indeed, since culture in the narrower sense has customarily been used to legitimate power – that is to say, used as ideology – this has in some sense always been so.

In our own time, the conflict between wider and narrower senses of culture has assumed a particularly paradoxical form. What has happened is that a local, fairly limited notion of culture has begun to proliferate universally. As Geoffrey Hartman points out in *The Fateful Question of Culture*, we now have 'camera culture, gun culture, service culture, museum culture, deaf culture, football culture . . . the culture of dependency, the culture of pain, the culture of amnesia, etc.'.[15] A phrase like 'café culture' means not just that people visit cafés but that some people visit them as a way of life, as they presumably do not in the case of their dentists. People who belong to the same place, profession or generation do not thereby form a culture; they do so only when they begin to share speech-habits, folk lore, ways of proceeding, frames of value, a collective self-image. It would be odd to see three people as forming a culture, but not three hundred or three million. The culture of a corporation includes its policy on sick leave but not its plumbing, its hierarchical parking arrangements but not the fact that it uses computers. It covers those aspects of it which embody a distinctive way of seeing the world, but not necessarily a unique way of seeing.

As far as breadth and narrowness go, this usage combines the worst of both worlds. 'Police culture' is both too nebulous and too exclusive, indiscriminately covering everything police officers get up to but implying that fire-fighters or flamenco dancers are a different breed altogether. If culture was once too rarefied a notion, it now has the flabbiness of a term which leaves out too little. But at the same time it has grown overspecialized, obediently reflecting the fragmentation of modern life rather than, as with a more classical concept of culture, seeking to repair it. 'With a self-consciousness never before attested (strongly stirred up by men of letters)', writes one commentator, 'each people now focuses on itself and squares off against the others in its language, its art, its literature, its philosophy, its civilisation, its "culture"'.[16] This could well be a description of, say, contemporary identity politics, though its date is actually 1927, and its author the French intellectual Julien Benda.

It is dangerous to claim that the idea of culture is nowadays in crisis, since when was it not? Culture and crisis go together like Laurel and Hardy. Even so, a momentous change has crept over the concept, which Hartman formulates as the conflict between culture and *a* culture, or, if one prefers, between Culture and culture. Traditionally, culture was a way in which we could sink our petty particularisms in some more capacious, all-inclusive medium. As a form of universal subjecthood, it signified those values which we shared simply by virtue of our common humanity. If culture-as-the-arts was important, it was because it distilled these values in conveniently portable form. In reading or viewing or listening, we suspended our empirical selves, with all their social, sexual and ethnic contingencies, and thereby became universal subjects ourselves. The standpoint of high culture, like that of the Almighty, was the view from everywhere and nowhere.

Since the 1960s, however, the word 'culture' has veered upon its axis to mean almost exactly the opposite. It now means the affirmation of a specific identity – national, sexual, ethnic, regional – rather than the transcendence of it. And since these identities all see themselves as suppressed, what was once conceived of as a realm of consensus has been transformed into a terrain of conflict. Culture, in brief, has passed over from being part of the solution to being part of the problem. It is no longer a means of resolving political strife, a higher or deeper dimension in which we can encounter one another purely as fellow humans; instead, it is part of the very lexicon of political conflict itself. 'Far from being a placid realm of Appollonian gentility', writes Edward Said, 'culture can even be a battleground on which causes expose themselves to the light of day and contend with one another'.[17] For the three forms of radical politics which have dominated the global agenda over the past few decades – revolutionary nationalism, feminism and ethnic struggle – culture as sign, image, meaning, value, identity, solidarity and self-expression is the very currency of political combat, not its Olympian alternative. In Bosnia or Belfast, culture is not just what you put on the cassette player; it is what you kill for. What culture loses in sublimity, it gains in practicality. In these circumstances, for both good and ill, nothing could be more bogus than the charge that culture is loftily remote from everyday life.

Some literary critics, faithfully reflecting this seismic shift of meaning, have accordingly scrambled out of Tudor drama into teenage magazines, or swapped their Pascal for pornography. There is something mildly unsettling in the spectacle of those trained to spot a pararhyme or a dactyl holding forth on the post-colonial subject, secondary narcissism or the Asiatic mode of production, matters which one might wish to see in rather less finely manicured hands. But the fact is that many of the so-called professional scholars, as is the way of treasonable clerks, have given up on such questions, thus dropping them into the lap of those who are perhaps least well trained to take them up. A literary education has many virtues, but systematic thought is not one of them. This move from literature to cultural politics is by no means simply incongruous, however, since what links these realms is the idea of subjectivity. Culture means the domain of social subjectivity – a domain which is wider than ideology but narrower than society, less palpable than the economy but more tangible than Theory. It is thus not illogical, though it may well be unwise, to believe that those trained in one science of subjectivity – literary criticism – are the best placed to discuss Hell's Angels' insignia or the semiotics of the shopping mall.

In the heyday of the European bourgeoisie, Literature played a key part in shaping this social subjectivity, and to be a literary critic was thus no politically inconsiderable role. It was certainly not for Johnson or Goethe, Hazlitt or Taine. The problem was that what gave most subtle expression to this subjective world – the arts – was also a rare phenomenon confined to a privileged minority; so that in the course of time it became hard to know whether as a critic one was utterly central or thoroughly superfluous. Culture in this sense was an intolerable paradox, at once supremely important and – since few did more than tip their hats to it – hardly important at all. One could always see these opposites as interdependent: the fact that the plebs and philistines had no time for culture was the most eloquent possible testimony to its value. But this placed the critic in a permanently dissenting posture, which is never the most comfortable place to live. The transition from Culture to culture solved this problem by preserving a dissident stance but combining it with a populist one. It was now a whole subculture which was critical, but within that way of life the arts played a largely affirmative role. One could thus be an outsider while savouring the delights of solidarity, as the prototypical *poète maudit* could not.

The radical nature of this shift in meaning can scarcely be understated. For culture in its more classical sense was not only meant to be non-political; it was actually set up as the very antithesis of politics. It was not just contingently non-political, but constitutively so. One can almost pinpoint the moment in English literary history, somewhere between Shelley and the early Tennyson, when 'poetry' becomes redefined as the very opposite of the public, prosaic, political, discursive, utilitarian. Perhaps every society carves out for itself a space in which, for one blessed moment, it may be free of these sublunary matters, and meditate instead on the very essence of the human. The names of this space are historically various: one could call it myth, religion, Idealist philosophy, or more recently Culture, Literature or the Humanities. Religion, which forges a relation between one's most intimate experience and the most fundamental questions of existence, such as why is there anything at all rather than just nothing, served this purpose supremely well in its day. Indeed it still does in pious, God-fearing societies such as the United States, where religion has an ideological prominence hard for a European to credit. Culture in the more specialized sense, fragile creature that it is, is far less robustly equipped to perform these functions; and when too much is expected of it – when it is asked to become a poor substitute for God, metaphysics or revolutionary politics – it may well start to betray pathological symptoms.

The inflation of culture is thus part of the story of a secularized age, as from Arnold onwards, Literature – of all things! – inherits the weighty ethical, ideological and even political tasks which were once entrusted to rather more technical or practical discourses. Industrial capitalism, with its rationalizing, secularizing bent, cannot help bringing its own metaphysical values into discredit, thus undermining the very foundation which that secular activity needs to legitimate itself. But if religion is losing its grip on the labouring masses, Culture is on hand as a second-rate surrogate; and it is this historic turning-point which Arnold's work marks. The idea is not wholly implausible: if religion offers cult, sensuous symbolism, social unity, collective identity, a combination of practical morality and spiritual idealism, and a link between the intellectuals and the populace, so does culture. Even so, culture is a lamentable alternative to religion for at least two reasons. In its narrower artistic sense it is confined to a paltry percentage of the population, and in its broader social sense it is exactly where men and women are least at one. Culture in this latter sense of religion, nationality, sexuality, ethnicity and the like is a field of ferocious contention; so that the more practical culture becomes, the less able it is to fulfil a conciliatory role, and the more conciliatory it is, the more ineffectual it grows.

Street-wise and disenchanted, postmodernism opts for culture as actual conflict rather than imaginary reconciliation. It is not of course original in this; Marxism, for one, had long anticipated it. Even so, it is hard to overestimate the scandalous effects of challenging the traditional idea of culture in this way. For that idea, as we have seen, was precisely constituted as the polar opposite of the social and material; and if the materialists can get their grubby paws even on this, then nothing is sacred any longer, least of all the sacred. Culture was where value itself had ducked for cover in a social order which was stonily indifferent to it; and if even this jealously patrolled enclave could come under fire from the historicists and materialists, then what was under siege seemed nothing less than human value itself. At least it seemed so to those who had long since ceased to discern value anywhere in the world outside the arts.

Nobody is much surprised when sociology or economics become 'political': one expects these inherently social inquiries to raise such questions. But to politicize culture would appear to deprive it of its very identity, and so to destroy it. It is no doubt for this reason that so much dust and heat has been generated in our time over that relatively harmless academic discourse known as literary theory. If there has been so much blood on the Senior Common Room carpets, some of it looking alarmingly like my own, then it can hardly be because anyone in the great scheme of things cares very much whether your approach to the poetry of Sir Walter Raleigh is feminist or Marxist, phenomenological or deconstructionist. These are not questions over which anyone in Whitehall or the White House is likely to lose sleep, or even matters which your college teachers are likely to be able to recall a year or so after you graduate. But societies are not so likely to look with such serene composure on those who seem to debilitate the very values by which they justify their power. And this, in effect, is one major meaning of the word 'culture'.

Even so, the postmodernists' sense of culture is not entirely remote from the universalist notion of it they so roundly denounce. For one thing, neither concept of culture is really self-critical. Just as high culture assumes like some cut-price retailer that it cannot be beaten for sheer value, so the artistic productions of West Yorkshire pigeon-fanciers are meant to affirm the value of West Yorkshire pigeon-fancying culture, not call it into doubt. For another thing, cultures in this postmodern sense are often concrete universals, localized versions of the very universalism they arraign. West Yorkshire pigeon-fanciers can no doubt be quite as conformist, exclusivist and autocratic as the larger world they inhabit. A pluralist culture must in any case be exclusivist, since it must shut out the enemies of pluralism. And since marginal communities tend to find the larger culture stiflingly oppressive, often with excellent reason, they can come to share the distaste for the habits of the majority which is an abiding feature of 'high' or aesthetic culture. The patrician and the dissenter can thus link hands over the heads of the petty bourgeoisie. From the standpoint of both elitist and nonconformist, suburbia looks a remarkably sterile place.

The rash of sub-cultures which go to make up the ironically entitled United States may testify at first glance to an alluring diversity. But since some of these sub-cultures are unified by their antagonism to others, they can succeed in transposing into local terms the global closure they detest in the classical notion of culture. At its worst, the result is a kind of pluralized conformism, in which the single universe of Enlightenment, with its self-sameness and coercive logic, is challenged by a whole series of mini-worlds displaying in miniature much the same features. Communitarianism is a case in point: instead of being tyrannized by a universal rationality, one is now hounded by one's next-door neighbours. Meanwhile, the ruling political system may take heart from the fact that it has not just one opponent, but a motley collection of disunited foes. If these sub-cultures protest against the alienations of modernity, they also reproduce them in their very fragmentation.

The apologists for such identity politics upbraid the guardians of aesthetic value for grossly inflating the importance of culture as art. Yet they themselves exaggerate the role of culture as politics. Culture is indeed integral to the kind of politics which postmodernism ranks high on its agenda, but that is because postmodernism favours just such sorts of politics. There are many other political contentions – strikes, anti-corruption campaigns, anti-war protests – to which culture is far less central, which is not to say that it is irrelevant. Yet a supposedly all-inclusive postmodernism has precious little to say about most of them. Cultural studies today, writes Francis Mulhern, 'leaves no room for politics beyond cultural practice, or for political solidarities beyond the particularisms of cultural difference'.[18] It fails to see not only that not all political issues are cultural, but that not all cultural differences are political. And in thus subordinating issues of state, class, political organization and the rest to cultural questions, it ends up rehearsing the prejudices of the very traditional *Kulturkritik* it rejects, which had little enough time itself for such mundane political matters. A distinctively American political agenda is universalized by a movement for which universalism is anathema. What *Kulturkritik* and modern-day culturalism also share is a lack of interest in what lies, politically speaking, beyond culture: the state apparatus of violence and coercion. Yet it is this, not culture, which is most likely in the end to defeat radical change.

Culture in this lower-case sense, as identity or solidarity, has some affinity with the anthropological sense of the term. But it is uneasy with what it sees as the normative bias of the latter, as well as with its nostalgic organicism. It is equally hostile to the normative bent of aesthetic culture, as well as to its elitism. Culture is no longer, in Matthew Arnold's exalted sense, a criticism of life, but the critique of a dominant or majority form of life by a peripheral one. Whereas high culture is the ineffectual opposite of politics, culture as identity is the continuation of politics by other means. For Culture, culture is benightedly sectarian, whereas for culture Culture is fraudulently disinterested. Culture is too ethereal for culture, and culture too earth-bound for Culture. We seem torn between an empty universalism and a blind particularism. If Culture is too unhoused and disembodied, culture is far too eager for a local habitation.

In *The Fateful Question of Culture*, Geoffrey Hartman, writing as a German Jewish emigré to the United States, refuses to idealize the notion of diaspora in the manner of the more callow postmodernists. 'Homelessness', he writes, 'is always a curse', a timely smack at those for whom nationlessness is next to godliness. But Hartman's background makes him equally sceptical of *volkisch* ideas of culture as integrity and identity, of that which appeases our ghostly longing to belong. The opposite of that local embodiment is the Jew: ungrounded, uprooted, sinisterly cosmopolitan, and thus a scandal to the *Kulturvolk*. Culture for postmodern theory may now be a dissident, minority affair, on the side of the Jew rather than the ethnic cleanser; yet the very word is tainted by the history of that cleansing. The word which signifies the most complex form of human refinement is also bound up, in the Nazi period, with the most unspeakable human debasement. If culture means the critique of empires, it also means the construction of them. And while culture in its most virulent forms celebrates some pure essence of group identity, Culture in its more mandarin sense, by disdainfully disowning the political as such, can be criminally complicit with it. As Theodor Adorno remarked, the ideal of Culture as absolute integration finds its logical expression in genocide. The two forms of culture are also alike in their claims to be non-political: high culture because it transcends such quotidian affairs, culture as collective identity because (in some, if by no means all, formulations) it cuts below politics rather than above them, in the textures of an instinctual mode of living.

Yet Culture as criminally complicit is only one side of the story. For one thing, there is a good deal in Culture which bears witness against genocide. For another thing, culture means not just an exclusivist identity, but those who collectively protest against such an identity. If there was a culture of Nazi genocide, there was also a culture of Jewish resistance. Since both senses of the word are ambivalent, neither can simply be mobilized against the other. The rift between Culture and culture is not a cultural one. It cannot be repaired simply by cultural means, as Hartman seems wistfully to hope. It has its roots in a material history – in a world which is itself torn between empty universalism and narrow particularism, the anarchy of global market forces and those cults of local difference which struggle to resist them. The more predatory the forces which lay siege to these local identities, the more pathological these identities become. This mighty combat leaves its imprint on other intellectual arguments too – on the battles between the moral and the ethical, the defenders of obligation and the champions of virtue, the Kantians and the communitarians. In all these cases, we are being pulled between the global reach of the mind and the constraints of our creatureliness.

One of our key words for the global reach of the mind is imagination, and perhaps no term in the literary-critical lexicon has been more unreservedly positive. Like 'community', 'imagination' is one of those words of which everyone approves, which is quite enough to make one darkly suspicious of it. The imagination is the faculty by which one can empathize with others – by which, for example, you can feel your way into the unknown territory of another culture. Indeed, into *any* other culture, since the faculty is universal in scope. But this leaves unresolved the question of where you, as opposed to they, are actually standing. In one sense, the imagination represents no position at all: it lives only in its vibrant fellow-feeling with others, and like Keats's 'negative capability' can enter sympathetically into any life-form. Like the Almighty, then, this quasi-divine capacity would seem to be at once all and nothing, everywhere and nowhere – a pure void of feeling with no firm identity of its own, feeding parasitically off the life-forms of others, yet transcendent of these life-forms in its very self-effacing capacity to enter into each of them in turn. The imagination thus centres and decentres at the same time, lending you a universal authority precisely by emptying you of distinctive identity. It is not to be reckoned up among the cultures it explores, since it is nothing but the activity of exploring them. The imagination thus has a promiscuousness which makes it something less than a stable identity, but also a mercurial many-sidedness to which such stable identities cannot rise. It is less an identity in itself than a knowledge of all identities, and so even more of an identity in the act of being somewhat less.

It is not hard to detect in this doctrine a liberal form of imperialism. In one sense, the West does not have a distinctive identity of its own, because it does not need one. The beauty of being a ruler is that one does not need to worry about who one is, since one deludedly believes that one already knows. It is other cultures which are different, while one's own form of life is the norm, and so scarcely a 'culture' at all. It is rather the standard by which other ways of life show up precisely *as* cultures, in all their charming or alarming uniqueness. It is not a question of Western culture but of Western civilization, a phrase which in one sense implies that the West is a particular way of life, and in another sense that it is simply the locus of a universal one. Imagination, or colonialism, means that what other cultures know is themselves, whereas what you know is them. If this makes you disturbingly less settled than they are, it also gives you a cognitive and political edge over them, the practical result of which is that they, too, are unlikely to be settled for long.

The colonialist encounter is thus one of Culture with culture – of a power which is universal, but thereby worryingly diffuse and unstable, with a state of being which is parochial but secure, at least until Culture gets its well-groomed hands on it. One can see the relevance of this to so-called multiculturalism. Society is made up of distinctive cultures, and in one sense is nothing but these; yet it is also a transcendent entity called 'society', which nowhere appears as a specific culture but which is the measure and matrix of them all. In this sense, society is rather like the work of art of classical aesthetics, which is similarly nothing beyond its unique particulars, but which is also their secret law. There is somewhere an implicit set of criteria which determine what is to count as a culture, what local rights they may be granted, and the like; but this concealed authority cannot itself be incarnate, since it is not itself a culture but the very conditions of possibility of one. Like the imagination, or the *folie de grandeur* of colonialism, it is that which inhabits all cultures, but only because it transcends them all.

There is, in fact, an internal link between the imagination and the West. Richard Rorty writes that

> Security and sympathy go together, for the same reasons that peace and economic productivity go together. The tougher things are, the more you have to be afraid of, the more dangerous your situation, the less you can afford the time or effort to think about what things might be like for people with whom you do not immediately identify. Sentimental education only works on people who can relax long enough to listen.[19]

From this notably hard-nosed materialist standpoint, you can be imaginative only if you are well heeled. It is affluence which liberates us from egoism. In a state of scarcity, we find it hard to rise above our material needs; only with the advent of a material surplus can we decentre ourselves into that imaginative surplus which is knowing what it feels like to be another. As with eighteenth-century 'civilization', but unlike nineteenth-century 'culture', spiritual and material progress here go hand in hand. Only the West today can be truly empathetic, since only it has the time and leisure to imagine itself as an Argentinian or an onion.

In one sense, this theory relativizes Culture: any affluent social order can attain to it, and if the West's affluence is historically contingent, then so are its civilized virtues. In another sense, the theory is to the spiritual realm what NATO is to the political one. Western civilization is not constrained by the peculiarities of a culture. It transcends all such cultures by having the capacity to understand them from the inside – understand them, like Schleiermacher's hermeneuticist, better than they do themselves – and so has the right to intervene for their own well-being into their affairs. The more Western culture universalizes itself, the less such intervention can be seen as one culture meddling with another, and the more plausibly it can be viewed as humanity putting its own house in order. For in the New World Order, as in the classical work of art, the stability of each component part is necessary to the flourishing of the whole. The Horatian tag 'Nothing human is alien to me' can now be rather less elegantly rendered as 'Any old backwater in the world is capable of threatening our profits'.

It is a mistake to believe, like Rorty, that downtrodden societies have too little time to imagine what others might be feeling. On the contrary, there are plenty of cases in which their downtroddenness is exactly what impels them to this sympathy. This has been known among other things as socialist internationalism, for which only by allying with similarly oppressed cultures might one's own bid for freedom have a hope of succeeding. If the pre-independent Irish took a lively interest in Egypt, India and Afghanistan, it was not because they could think of no better way of frittering away their leisure time. Colonialism is a great breeder of imaginative sympathy, since it throws together the most oddly assorted cultures in roughly the same conditions. It is also a mistake to imagine that one culture can dialogue with another only by virtue of some special faculty which both possess over and above their local peculiarities. This is because there is no such thing as local peculiarities. All localities are porous and open-ended, overlap with other such contexts, betray family resemblances with apparently remote situations, and shade off ambiguously into their equally shady surroundings.

But it is also because you do not need to leap out of your skin to know what another is feeling; indeed there are times when you need rather to burrow more deeply into it. A society which has suffered colonization, for example, has only to consult its own 'local' experience to feel solidarity with another such colony. Of course there will be key differences; but the early twentieth-century Irish did not need to resort to some mysterious intuitive faculty to know something of how the early twentieth-century Indians felt. It is those who fetishize cultural differences who are the reactionaries here. It was by belonging to their own cultural history, not by putting it temporarily on ice, that these societies were able to go beyond it. I do not understand you by ceasing to be myself, since then there would be nobody to do the understanding. And your understanding of me is not a matter of reduplicating in yourself what I am feeling, an assumption which might well raise thorny issues of how you come to leap the ontological barrier between us. To believe this is to assume that I am in perfect possession of my own experience, luminously transparent to myself, and the only problem is how you are to have access to this self-transparency. But I am not in fact in full possession of my own experience; I can sometimes be quite mistaken about what I am feeling, let alone thinking; you might quite often understand me better than I can myself; and the way you understand me is pretty much the way I understand myself. Understanding is not a form of empathy. I do not understand a chemical formula by empathizing with it. I am not incapable of sympathy for a slave because I have never been enslaved myself, or unable to appreciate the sufferings involved in being a woman because I am not a woman myself. To believe so is to make a crudely Romantic mistake about the nature of understanding. But such Romantic prejudices, to judge from some forms of identity politics, are clearly alive and well.

Whatever these empathetic errors, it is true that Western culture shows a lamentable failure to imagine other cultures. Nowhere is this more obvious than in the phenomenon of aliens. What is really sinister about aliens is just how unalien they are. They are dismal testimony to our inability to conceive of life-forms radically different from our own. They may have bulbous heads and triangular eyes, speak in a chillingly robotic monotone or emit a strong stench of sulphur, but otherwise they look much like Tony Blair. Creatures capable of travelling for light years turn out to have heads, limbs, eyes and voices. Their spacecraft can navigate black holes but tend to crash in the Nevada desert. Despite being built in galaxies inconceivably remote from us, these ships leave ominous burn marks on our soil. Their occupants take a curiously familiar interest in examining human genitals, and tend to deliver vague, waffling messages about the need for world peace, like a UN Secretary-General. They peep into kitchen windows in their inconceivably alien fashion, and take an excited extra-terrestrial interest in false teeth. In fact, as immigration officers might do well to note, creatures with whom we can communicate are by definition not alien. The real aliens are those who have been sitting in our laps for centuries without our noticing.

There is, finally, one other link between culture and power. No political power can survive satisfactorily by naked coercion. It will lose too much ideological credibility, and so prove dangerously vulnerable at times of crisis. But in order to secure the consent of those it governs, it needs to know them more intimately than as a set of graphs or statistical tables. Since true authority involves the internalizing of the law, it is on human subjectivity itself, in all its apparent freedom and privacy, that power seeks to impress itself. To govern successfully, it must therefore understand men and women in their secret desires and aversions, not just in their voting habits or social aspirations. If it is to regulate them from the inside, it must also imagine them from the inside. And no cognitive form is more adroit at mapping the complexities of the heart than artistic culture. So it is that, as the nineteenth century draws on, the realist novel becomes a source of social knowledge incomparably more graphic and intricate than any positivist sociology. High culture is not some ruling-class conspiracy; if it sometimes fulfils this cognitive function, it can also sometimes disrupt it. But works of art which seem most innocent of power, in their sedulous attention to the motions of the heart, may serve power for precisely that reason.

Even so, we may come to look back with affectionate nostalgia on these regimes of knowledge, which for the Foucaultians seem the last word in insidious oppression. Ruling powers do not plump for coercion if they can secure consensus; but as the gap between the rich and poor of the world steadily widens, the prospect now looms for the coming millennium of a progressively bunkered, authoritarian capitalism, beleaguered in a decaying social landscape by increasingly desperate enemies from within and without, finally abandoning all pretence of consensual government for a brutally forthright defence of privilege. There are many forces which may resist this cheerless prospect, but culture does not rank particularly high among them.

3

Culture Wars

The phrase 'culture wars' suggests pitched battles between populists and elitists, custodians of the canon and devotees of *difference*, dead white males and the unjustly marginalized. The clash between Culture and culture, however, is no longer simply a battle of definitions, but a global conflict. It is a matter of actual politics, not just academic ones. It is not just a tussle between Stendhal and *Seinfeld*, or between those churls on the English department corridor who study line-endings in Milton and the bright young things who write books on masturbation. It is part of the shape of the world politics of the new millennium. Though culture, as we shall see, is still not politically sovereign, it is intensely relevant to a world in which the joint wealth of the three richest individuals is equal to the combined wealth of 600 million of the poorest. It is just that the culture wars which matter concern such questions as ethnic cleansing, not the relative merits of Racine and soap operas.

In an apt phrase, Fredric Jameson writes of 'NATO high culture'.[1] Why so? NATO, after all, does not produce high culture as it produces mission statements, and if NATO high culture is just another way of saying 'Western culture', then there is a good deal of high culture in the world that is not Western at all. Fine arts and fine living are not the monopoly of the West. Nor can high culture these days be confined to traditional bourgeois art, covering as it does a much more diverse, market-driven field.[2] 'High' certainly does not mean non-commercial, nor does 'mass' necessarily mean non-radical. The boundary between 'high' and 'low' culture has also been eroded by such genres as film, which has managed to chalk up an impressive array of masterpieces while appealing to almost everyone.

In any case, there is a lot in Western high culture which runs counter to the priorities of NATO. Dante, Goethe, Shelley and Stendhal cannot be dragooned into the literary wing of a military alliance without a good deal of rewriting. Those radicals for whom high culture is *ipso facto* reactionary forget that much of it is well to the left of the World Bank. It is not on the whole the content of such culture that radicals should complain of, but its function. What is objectionable is that it has been used as the spiritual badge of a privileged group, not the fact that Alexander Pope was a Tory or Balzac a monarchist. Much popular culture is just as conservative. It would be hard to argue that the values of canonical literature as a whole support the political establishment. Homer was not a liberal humanist, Virgil did not champion bourgeois values, Shakespeare put in a good word for radical egalitarianism, Samuel Johnson cheered on popular insurrection in the Caribbean, Flaubert despised the middle classes and Tolstoy had no time for private property.

What matters is not the works themselves but the way they are collectively construed, ways which the works themselves could hardly have anticipated. Taken together, they are offered as evidence of the timeless unity of the human spirit; of the superiority of the imaginative to the actual; of the inferiority of ideas to feelings; of the truth that the individual stands at the centre of the universe; of the relative unimportance of public as against interpersonal life, or of the practical as against the contemplative, and other such modern prejudices. But one could just as well construe them quite differently. It is not Shakespeare who is worthless, just some of the social uses to which his work has been put. An assault on the institution of monarchy need not imply that the queen herself is a depraved wretch. In any case, many of the advocates of Dante and Goethe have never read a word of them. In this sense, too, it is not the content of such culture which matters, but what it signifies. And what it signifies today, among other more positive things, is the defence of a certain 'civility' against fresh forms of so-called barbarism. But since these fresh forms of barbarism, paradoxically, can also be seen as particular *cultures*, the Culture versus culture polarity comes into being.

The point about Culture is that it is cultureless: its values are not those of any particular form of life, simply of human life as such. It may well be that a specific historical culture known as Europe is the spot where this humanity chose to incarnate itself most fully, but one might always claim that the historical reasons for this were purely contingent. In any case, since the values of Culture are universal but not *abstract*, they could not thrive without some kind of local habitation. In this sense one can contrast Culture with Reason, which also transcends particular cultures but which does so because it is inherently unbound by place or time. There could not be a peculiarly Korean version of the Kantian categorical imperative. Culture, by contrast, has an ironic relation to its historical *milieu*: if it needs that setting to realize itself, it is also Culture only because it surpasses it towards the universal.

In this sense, Culture itself is a kind of Romantic symbol, as the infinite takes on a local incarnation. It is the still point of the turning world, at which time and eternity, the senses and the spirit, motion and immobility, intersect. It was Europe's good fortune to be singled out by *Geist* as the place where it took on flesh, rather as it was planet Earth's good fortune to be selected as the spot where God would opt to become human. In interpreting Culture, then, just as in interpreting the symbol, we must operate a kind of double-coding and grasp it as at once itself and something else, the product of a specific civilization yet also of universal spirit. Just as it would be an unskilful reading of, say, *Madame Bovary* to find in it no more than the tale of a bored provincial housewife, so it would be an obtuse reading of Western Culture to treat it simply as the record of a specific, culture-bound experience. Indeed to claim that a work belongs to high culture is to claim among other things that it has an inherent portability, a sort of built-in detachability from its context, as bus tickets and political leaflets do not. What forestalls such a reductive reading is aesthetic form, which shapes this local material into something of wider purport, and which thus provides the reader with a model of what he himself is to do if he is to receive the work as high culture. Just as form links the elements of a work into a greater whole, with no damage to their particularity, so Culture signifies a link between a specific civilization and universal humanity.

Like all the most effective forms of power, high culture presents itself simply as a form of moral persuasion. It is, among other things, a way in which a governing order fashions an identity for itself in stone, script and sound, and its effect is to intimidate as well as to inspire. Like the doorkeeper of a Pall Mall club, its role is not simply to let people in. But its resources are by no means confined to these social functions, and to imagine that they were would be the most naive form of genetic fallacy. It would also be to overestimate the power of high culture, and thus ironically to endorse an idealist view of it. High culture is one of the least significant of ideological weapons, which is the kernel of truth of the illusion that it is entirely free of ideology. It is inestimably less important than education or sexuality. There would be no justification for political radicals working in this field unless they found themselves there already, or were especially skilled at it.

Given Culture's own self-understanding, then, it is not difficult to see what it finds so scandalous about cultures. For cultures are blatantly particular, resonant of nothing but themselves, and without these differences they would disappear. To be sure, this contrast between universal Culture and specific cultures is ultimately deceptive, since pure difference would be indistinguishable from pure identity. A life-world which really did establish its distinction from every other would become a kind of universal. It would be like those marginal or minority cultures today which reject the 'tyranny' of universal consensus but sometimes end up reproducing a microcosmic version of it in their own closed, autonomous, strictly coded worlds. All the same, there is an important difference between the two versions of culture when it comes to the question of particularity. Culture as identity is averse to both universality and individuality; instead, it values collective particularity. From the viewpoint of Culture, culture perversely seizes upon the accidental particulars of existence – gender, ethnicity, nationality, social origin, sexual tendency and the like – and converts them into the bearers of necessity.

What Culture itself cherishes is not the particular but that very different animal, the individual. Indeed it sees a direct relation between the individual and the universal. It is in the uniqueness of a thing that the world spirit can be most intimately felt; but to disclose the essence of a thing means stripping away its accidental particulars. What constitutes my own self-identity is the self-identity of the human spirit. What makes me what I am is my essence, which is the species to which I belong. Culture is itself the spirit of humanity individuating itself in specific works; and its discourse links the individual and the universal, the quick of the self and the truth of humanity, without the mediation of the historically particular. Indeed nothing could more closely resemble the universe than that which is purely itself, with no external relations. The universal is not just the opposite of the individual, but the very paradigm of it.

It is in the very *quidditas* of a thing, its peculiar pith and taste, that we are in the presence of that which transcends all mere particulars. Individuality is the medium of the universal, while particulars are purely random. The medieval distinction between essence and accident is thus replayed, this time as a confrontation between Culture and culture. The former, in universalizing the individual, realizes its true identity; the latter is just a contingent way of life, an accident of place and time which could always have been otherwise. It is not, as Hegel might have said, 'in the Idea'. High culture thus sets up a direct circuit between individual and universal, by-passing all arbitrary particulars in the process. What else is the artistic canon, a collection of irreducibly individual works which testify in their very uniqueness to the common spirit of humanity? Or think of the ethics of liberal humanism, for which I am most peculiarly myself when I rise above my prosaic particularity, perhaps through the transfigurative power of art, to become the bearer of a universal humanity. Art recreates individual things in the form of their universal essences, and in doing so makes them inimitably themselves. In the process, it converts them from contingency to necessity, dependency to freedom. What resists this alchemical process is purged away as so much particularist dross.

There is a modern, ironic version of this doctrine, which can be found in the work of Richard Rorty.[3] As a good pragmatist, Rorty acknowledges that the cultural tradition he himself endorses – Western, bourgeois, liberal, enlightened, social democratic-to-postmodern reformism – is purely contingent. It could always have happened otherwise, and there was no doubt even less necessity for him personally to have been born into it. But he embraces it as a universal good even so. It has no universal foundation, but a religious fundamentalist would nevertheless be well advised to adopt it. What Rorty does, in short, is to raise contingency to universality without erasing its contingency, thus reconciling his historicism with his absolutizing of Western ideology. Indeed his historical relativism is the very ground of his absolutism. If no culture can be metaphysically underwritten, then there can be no rational grounds on which to choose among them – in which case, like the ancient Sophists, you might as well choose the one in which you happen to find yourself. But since there is no rational motive for this choice, it becomes, like the existential *acte gratuit*, a kind of absolute in itself. For some other pragmatists, by contrast, one cannot logically speak of choosing the culture in which one finds oneself, since the fact that one is there in the first place is the ground of one's 'choice'. Rorty's raising of the contingent to the universal is, one might claim, the most typical gesture of ideology; it is just that he hopes its ironic self-awareness will redeem it from this fate. In fact, all he has done is to flee a 'modernist' sense of ideology, for which one is not in possession of the truth, for a postmodernist one, for which one knows that what one is doing is false without ceasing to do it. The epistemology of illusion gives way to the epistemology of cynicism.

If individuality erases the particular in its essentialism, universality disposes of it in its abstraction. But this abstraction is perfectly at one with individuality. Indeed the spirit of humanity exists only in its individual incarnations, for which another name is poetry. High culture is thus the sworn foe of generality. It is not only an alternative to rational argument but an alternative conception of reason as such, one which spurns utility and abstraction for the feel and flavour of things. It was born at a time when abstract rationalism was becoming a weapon in the hands of the political left, and is thus an implicit rebuke to it. But if it is wedded to the individual, it is equally hostile to the sheerly particular – to those turbulent local interests which have yet to be subsumed under the law of the whole.

In fact, what the universal commonly does is seize upon the historically particular and project it as an eternal truth. A contingent history – that of the West – becomes the history of humanity as such. However, as Kate Soper has reminded us, 'universalist discourses about "humanity" are indeed at risk of introducing an ethnocentric bias into their view of what is common to us all; but discourses that would deny any shared structure of cognition, need and affectivity may also license a callous political neglect of the sufferings and deprivations of others'.[4] Universality is not, in other words, to be universally abjured. Postmodern thinkers should be properly anti-universalist on this score, distinguishing in the true spirit of pluralism those uses of the concept which are pragmatically fruitful from those which are not. If universality means that the Tungus people of eastern Siberia find themselves faithfully reflected in the work of Noel Coward, it should be rejected; if it means that the Tungus experience pain pretty much in the way that Germans do, it should be embraced. The typical Westerner, in the words of the anthropologist Ruth Benedict, may indeed 'accept without more ado the equivalence of human nature and his own cultural standards',[5] but we should recall that such errors are not peculiar to the West. As Benedict goes on to point out, there are many cultures for which the stranger is defined as non-human. One should not be ethnocentric about ethnocentricity.

There is a political correlative of the unity of individual and universal, known as the nation-state. The prime political form of modernity is itself an uneasy negotiation between individual and universal. To be plucked from the casualities of time and raised to the status of necessity, nations require the universalizing medium of the state. The hyphen in the term 'nation-state' thus signifies a link between culture and politics, the ethnic and the engineered.[6] The nation is amorphous stuff, which needs to be shaped by the state into unity; its unruly elements will thus be reconciled under a single sovereignty. And since this sovereignty is an emanation of Reason itself, the local is thus raised to the universal. But since this process is happening all over the world, given that few movements are more international than nationalism, the nation is elevated to global status in this sense too.

Membership of the tribe thus yields to citizenship of the world. But since one has to be a citizen of the world on some particular spot, given the constraints of our creatureliness, the local is given fresh meaning rather than just discarded. This, at least, is the aim of those Romantic nationalisms which seek the universal through the specific, and which see each nation as achieving it in its own distinctive way. Some Enlightenment models of the nation, by contrast, can be rather more brusque about local differences, despising such idiosyncrasy as an obstacle to universal freedom. Regionality is thus to be crushed beneath rationality. But if culture as an idea surges to the fore at this time, it is largely because actual cultures are performing a more ambitious role on the world political stage. Cultures are now becoming the basis of the nation-state, but a nation-state which nevertheless transcends them.

Political states differ from each other, but these differences are not always of world-shaking significance. What matters is that you are a citizen of a state which allows you civil liberties, not the particular mechanisms by which this is secured. As far as that goes, being French is no more inherently desirable than being Chilean. Culturally speaking, however, belonging to one nation rather than another is so vitally important that people are quite often prepared to kill or die over the question. If politics is what unifies, culture is what differentiates. This preference for one cultural identity rather than another is a-rational, in the sense that opting to belong to a democracy rather than a dictatorship is not. Racism and chauvinism, which try to justify such a preference on the grounds of the superiority of one cultural identity over another, are just such spurious attempts to rationalize it. But the fact that a choice of cultural identity is *a*-rational is no argument against it, any more than it is an argument against one's choice of sexual partner. There is nothing necessarily benighted about enjoying the company of people of one's own kind, as long as this does not imply a value-judgement (these people are innately superior to others), exclude other groups, or obscure the fact that learning to be with people not of one's own kind is a precious part of one's education. In any case, our cultural allegiances, whether to those of our own group or to others, are not necessarily *ir*rational because they are *a*-rational. We can sometimes give reasons for such preferences, as we can give reasons for our choice of partner. It is just that such preferences are not in the end reducible to those reasons, as is plain from the fact that someone else may see why you love your partner without loving him herself.

The nation-state does not unqualifiedly celebrate the idea of culture. On the contrary, any particular national or ethnic culture will come into its own only through the unifying principle of the state, not under its own steam. Cultures are intrinsically incomplete, and need the supplement of the state to become truly themselves. This is why, at least for Romantic nationalism, each ethnic people has a right to its own state simply by virtue of being a distinct people, since the state is the supreme way in which its ethnic identity can be realized. A state which contained more than one culture would thus inevitably fail to do justice to them all. It is this assumption of an internal link between culture and politics which has helped to wreak so much havoc in the modern world, as different national groups vie for sovereignty of the same piece of territory. In fact, what originally distinguishes the idea of nationalism is not so much a claim to territorial sovereignty – a claim familiar enough, after all, to aboriginal warriors and Renaissance princes – but to the sovereignty of a specific people, who happen to occupy a particular patch. It is republicanism, not soil, which is primarily at stake here. But if what prevents the self-determination of the people is the presence on their soil of a colonial power, then it is easy to see how democratic republican arguments can become displaced into nationalist talk of race, motherland and territorial integrity.

What are ideally united in the nation-state, then, are *ethos* and abstract rights, ethnic uniqueness and political universality, *Gemeinschaft* and *Gesellschaft*, the common folk and the cosmopolitan intelligentsia. Ideally, local pieties, customs and affinities – culture, in a word – are preserved, but a political unity supervenes upon them. In reality, things are rather less harmonious. We are now called on to reinvent at a higher, more universal level the kind of solidarity we once supposedly enjoyed in the more parochial realm of culture. We must now learn to invest in the political sphere itself all those energies which we had previously reserved for kith and kin, the spirit of place and the genealogy of the tribe. The nation-state is the place where a potentially universal community of free, equal citizens can be instantiated – rather as the Romantic symbol is a concretization of the world spirit. It was the *patria* which hailed you as a French revolutionary citizen; but the *patria* was the locus of a Reason and Liberty which were by no means exclusively French. To be sure, only certain cultures – those which had already evolved beyond a primitive clannishness to some semblance of civility – would prove hospitable to these higher political forms. There would always be those Calibans on whose nature nurture would never stick. And there was no denying that this delicate equipoise of culture and politics was hardly an easy one to maintain. For one thing, hardly any political state clings to the contours of some distinct ethnicity. And culture is more the product of politics than politics is the dutiful handmaiden of culture. For another thing, the state can represent the unity of a culture only by repressing its internal contradictions. Quite how one represents contradiction is a troubling question, not least if one believes with Marx that the political state is itself a product of contradiction. Only by some curious homoeopathy, then, could the state be the cure for a condition of which it is itself symptomatic.

There are other difficulties as well. Civic or political nationalism sometimes finds it convenient to rally ethnic nationalism to its standard, as, for example, the unity of the modern post-colonial state is underpinned by a mythology of origins. But the more the universal-rational form of the state seeks to strengthen its authority by raiding the resources of ethnic culture, the more it risks its universality being undermined by them. 'State' and 'nation' are not so easily hyphenated, moving as they do at different levels. If the civic forms of the state need to conscript ethnic intensities, they also need to keep them in check. It is on the whole the nation, rather than the state, that men and women will die for, but from the state's viewpoint this impulse is as gratifyingly tenacious as it is alarmingly fanatical. Culture is in some sense more primordial than politics, but also less pliable. Men and women are more likely to take to the streets over cultural and material issues rather than purely political ones – the cultural being what concerns one's spiritual identity, and the material one's physical one. It was through the nation-state that we were being constituted as citizens of the world; but it was hard to see how this form of political identity could furnish motives as deep-seated as cultural ones.

It is true that anyone who considers that a global identity is too abstract an affair for this purpose has obviously never encountered a Roman Catholic. And if the new citizen of the world today is the corporate executive, it is also the ecological campaigner. It is with ecological politics above all that the links between the local and the global, a Romantic *pietas* of place and an Enlightenment universality, have been most firmly resoldered. In any case, many men and women have struggled and sometimes died in the name of international solidarity. Communities are not just local affairs. It is hard, even so, to imagine at present men and women throwing themselves on the barricades crying 'Long live the European Union!'. The problem is that our modes of politics and our forms of culture have come adrift, in an age when one ideal resolution of the two – the nation-state – is increasingly under siege. One can speak, for example, of 'corporation culture', but this simply means a way of doing things typical of corporations, not a culture which will legitimate this way of doing things in popular consciousness.

The vision of classical nationalism was of a world made up of unique, self-determining particulars known as nations, each of which would carve out its own distinctive path to self-realization. This way of seeing thus bears a remarkable affinity to aesthetic thought. Indeed it was the aesthetic artefact, of all things, which was modernity's other great solution to one of its own most obdurate problems: the vexed relation between individual and universal. It is no doubt for this reason that aesthetic questions crop up so often in a society which has less and less time for art. What the work of art promised was a whole new way of conceiving of the relationship at issue, refusing both empty universality and blind particularity by grasping the work of art as that peculiar kind of totality which exists only in and through its sensuous particulars. The universal 'law' of the artefact was no more than the configuration of its component parts. Obedience to the law is here true freedom: the artwork's general law or form is what allows each of its parts to be freely self-determining, since it is no more than the effect of their joint activity. Here, then, was a world at once sensuous and quasi-conceptual, where abstract form was nothing but an articulation of unique individuals. Each of these individuals determined itself in and through its determining of the others, thus foreshadowing a kind of political utopia. If culture could be harmonized with global politics by the nation-state, Culture could equally reconcile the universal and the specific.

But if culture laid the basis of the nation-state, it now threatens to scupper it. The national unity which is sealed by Culture is shattered by culture. The Romantic-nationalist myth of the unity of culture and politics, which served a good many nation-states remarkably well in its day, not to speak of a good many anti-colonial movements, cannot easily survive the emergence of multiculturalism. In one sense, to be sure, multiculturalism is simply a later ironic turn of the same history. Secure in their singular cultural identity, nation-states created colonial subjects whose descendants then joined them as immigrants, thus jeopardizing the cultural unity which had helped to make empire possible in the first place. The unified culture of the nation-state was thus endangered from 'below' just as it was being simultaneously assailed from 'above'. Transnational capitalism weakens national cultures, just as it does national economies, by cosmopolitanizing them. As Jean-François Lyotard writes: 'one listens to reggae, watches a western, eats McDonald's food for lunch and local cuisine for dinner, wears Paris perfume in Tokyo and "retro" clothes in Hong Kong'.[7]

Whereas the migrant travels the world, the world travels to the cosmopolitan. The migrant cannot go home, whereas the cosmopolitan has no home to go to.

If migration is the popular form of multiculturalism, cosmopolitanism is its elitist version. Both are products of the same global economic system. But since transnational capitalism also breeds isolation and anxiety, uprooting men and women from their traditional attachments and pitching their identity into chronic crisis, it fosters, by way of reaction, cultures of defensive solidarity at the very time that it is busy proliferating this brave new cosmopolitanism. The more avant-garde the world waxes, the more archaic it grows. As hybridity spreads, so do the cries of heresy. For every waft of Parisian perfume in Tokyo, one can find a young Nazi thug or a middle-aged communitarian philosopher. Once the mould of the nation-state is cracked, types of cultural politics which never quite fitted that framework, not least sexual politics, are able to thrive. But as cosmopolitanism locks horns with communalism, the one with too little identity and the other with too much, the temporary resolutions of nationalism and aesthetics begin to fall apart into a 'bad' universalism on the one hand and a 'bad' particularism on the other. At the same time, culture and politics begin to change relation.

This can be seen among other places in post-colonial theory. If the nation-state was always a spurious harmony of culture and politics, revolutionary nationalism was quite a different affair. Here culture could become a transformative political force, in what remains the most spectacularly successful radical movement of modern history. Post-colonialism, as the word suggests, comes in the wake of this historic moment, once revolutionary nationalism has given birth to a rash of nation-states. It is thus, chronologically speaking, post-nationalist, post-revolutionary, even at times post-ideological and post-political. But this chronological fact, for which post-colonialist theory itself can hardly be blamed, can blend conveniently with its own predilection for questions of cultural identity rather than questions of radical politics, as a post-historical north encounters a post-colonial south. Culture, in short, can come to oust the politics with which it was previously so closely bound up.

Our culture wars, then, are at least three-way: between culture as civility, culture as identity, and culture as commercial or postmodern. One might define these types more pithily as excellence, *ethos* and economics. As Adorno might have said had he lived to see them, they are the torn thirds of a freedom to which they fail to add up. The distinction is an unstable one, since postmodernism and the more enlightened forms of identity politics are in many ways allied. But what matters here is the difference between, say, the White Christian Riflemen of Montana and Michael Jackson. This is hardly a difference in degrees of sanity, but between culture as identity, and postmodern culture in the sense of the consumerist culture of advanced capitalism. (To call it 'late' capitalism is somewhat presumptuous, since we have no idea how late it is.) Both of these senses of culture are challenged by culture as civility. Culture as civility is not just an aesthetic affair: it holds, rather, that the value of a whole way of life is embodied in certain accomplished artefacts. If the canon matters, it is because it is the touchstone of civility in general, not just because of its inherent merit. It is not a question of art usurping social life, but of art indicating a fineness of living to which society itself should aspire. Art defines what we live for, but it is not art for which we live. The case is thus open and closed together: how generous to see art as in the service of life, and how parochial to imagine that art alone defines what is worth living for!

What has happened in our day is not just that this sense of culture is locked in ferocious dispute with culture as identity. There was always a quarrel between liberal and communalist versions of culture. It is rather that it has been mapped on to some of the major political conflicts of our time, including those between the north and south of the globe. Culture as aesthetic and culture as anthropological now constitute not just an academic quarrel but a geopolitical axis. They represent, in effect, the difference between the West and its others. But it is also, more generally, the difference between liberal civilization and all those more corporate forms – nationalism, nativism, identity politics, neo-fascism, religious fundamentalism, family values, communitarian traditions, the world of eco-warriors and New Ageists – with which it does battle. To see this as a conflict between 'developed' and 'underdeveloped' regions is in fact deeply misleading. Many of these corporate forms are reactions to that larger corporatism we know as transnational capitalism, whose own culture can be quite as claustrophobic as a prayer meeting or a rifle club. And if liberal values versus culture as solidarity is a matter of north versus south, then it is hard to know what to make of, say, Islamic liberalism in its rejection of US Christian fundamentalism, or Indian socialism in its opposition to European racism. The north of the globe has no monopoly on enlightened values, whatever it likes to consider in its more smugly self-righteous moments. Even so, the running battle between these two senses of culture has now become a global affair.

From the viewpoint of Culture, what a gay rights group and a neo-fascist cell have in common is in a sense as striking as their political differences. Both define culture as collective identity rather than as critique, as a distinctive way of life rather than a form of value relevant to any way of life whatsoever. To this extent, Culture appears more pluralistic than, say, a gay rights group or a trade union. In fact, the diversity of Culture is a little deceptive, since the principles it defends are often few and absolute. And a tolerant plurality is exactly what gay rights groups exist to promote. It is true that they derive this creed in part from Culture itself, which may be oppressive in form but can be enlightened enough in content. Culture as civility includes the liberal, emancipatory tenets of which identity politics are the late, often reluctant inheritors. There can be no political emancipation for our time which is not at some level indebted to the Enlightenment, however resentful of this parentage it may be. Those who have been excluded, however, are bound to appear uncivilized, since their fight for recognition tends to assume corporate or militant forms distasteful to liberal cultivation. It follows that the more vociferously they protest against their exclusion, the more justified that exclusion appears. One should remember, however, that it was the less admirable aspects of liberal cultivation which forced them into this militancy in the first place. Cultures struggling for recognition cannot usually afford to be intricate or self-ironizing, and the responsibility for this should be laid at the door of those who suppress them. But intricacy and self-irony are virtues even so. That someone in the process of being lowered into a snakepit cannot be ironic is a critical comment on his situation, not on irony. The fact that Culture can afford such virtues, whereas culture often cannot, makes no difference to this fact. We would know if a cultural identity had been securely established by its ability to engage in irony and self-criticism.

The paradox of identity politics, in short, is that one needs an identity in order to feel free to get rid of it. The only thing worse than having an identity is not having one. Lavishing a lot of energy on affirming one's identity is preferable to feeling that one has no identity at all, but being in neither situation is even more desirable. Like all radical politics, identity politics are self-abolishing: one is free when one no longer needs to bother oneself too much about who one is. In this sense, the end is at odds with the means, as it is in traditional class politics. A classless society can be achieved only by taking class identifications seriously, not by a liberal pretence that they do not exist. The most uninspiring kind of identity politics are those which claim that an already fully fledged identity is being repressed by others. The more inspiring forms are those in which you lay claim to an equality with others in being free to determine what you might wish to become. Any authentic affirmation of difference thus has a universal dimension.

If it is the less admirable aspects of liberal cultivation which has forced gay rights groups and their ilk into militancy, the reverse is also true. It is the proliferation of cultures which has forced Culture into a discomforting self-awareness. For civility works best when it is the invisible colour of everyday life, and for it to feel forced to objectify itself is to concede far too much to its critics. Culture then risks being relativized as just another culture. This is particularly observable at the present time. Western civilization, which has now embarked on a more ambitiously aggressive foreign policy, needs some spiritual legitimation for this project at just the time when it is threatening to come apart at the cultural seams. The more it uproots whole communities, breeds widespread poverty and unemployment, undermines traditional belief systems and creates great tidal waves of migration, the more these predatory policies throw up a series of defensive, militant sub-cultures which splinter Western society from within. They also engender similar forces abroad. This is not to see all so-called identity politics as a mere negative response to social instability. On the contrary, some forms of it are simply the latest phase of what Raymond Williams has called the 'long revolution'. Even so, the result is that Western culture is disabled at the very moment when it needs to affirm its universal authority. Once its values are challenged, Culture can no longer be invisible. The ideal unity of Culture is more and more at odds with the conflict of cultures, and can no longer offer to resolve them. Hence the celebrated crisis of Culture of our time.

But there are other difficulties too. It is hard for a way of life whose priorities are secular, rationalist, materialist and utilitarian to produce a culture adequate to these values. For are not these values inherently *anti*-cultural? This, to be sure, was always a headache for industrial capitalism, which was never really able to spin a persuasive cultural ideology out of its own philistine practices. Instead, it was forced for this purpose to exploit the symbolic resources of the Romantic humanist tradition, and in doing so betrayed the discrepancy between its utopian ideal and its sordid actuality. Culture, then, is not only too unitary a notion for an inevitably fragmented capitalism, but too high-minded a one as well. It is in danger of drawing attention to the farcical gap between its own earnest spiritual rhetoric and the unlovely prose of everyday life. A European Union anthem to the Almighty would be merely embarrassing. Yet as we have seen already, Culture is fatally enfeebled once it comes adrift from its roots in religion, even if clinging to those roots means consigning itself to irrelevance.

It is not out of the question to imagine a Europe under siege recasting itself 'in the image of a Holy Alliance', a 'rejuvenated Christendom' or 'White Man's Club', as Aijaz Ahmad has suggested.[8] If Culture must now unify a somewhat patchwork, quarrelsome West against what seems to it to be culture in all the wrong senses, then the revival of a common classical, Christian, liberal-humanist heritage may well prove a way of repelling the marauding barbarians from beyond. Culture in the sense of the fine arts could be expected to play a significant role in any such reinvention, which is why debates over Virgil and Dante are by no means just academicist affairs. Alliances like NATO and the European Union usually need to cement their bonds with something a little thicker than bureaucracy, common political goals or shared economic interests, not least when they are facing Islamic enemies for whom culture in the spiritual sense is utterly vital. In this context, wranglings over Great Books courses assume a new significance. And religion, after all, is the single most powerful ideological force which human history has ever witnessed.

The poet Seamus Heaney protests in an interview that

> if you take out, almost in a military sense, the forms of the (European) inheritance, if you take out Greek, Hellenic, Judaic culture – after all, the literary and artistic culture is almost coterminous with our discovery of moral culture, I mean justice, freedom, beauty, love: they are in the drama of Greece, they are in the holy books of Judea – and if you take out these things, what do you put in their stead?[9]

Heaney is right to defend these precious traditions against those who would junk them as so much ideology; but he speaks as though European culture is a homogeneous heritage, without negativity or contradiction. If Europe is indeed the cradle of so much civilization, then it might at least have the decency to apologize for it. For it is of course a history of slavery, genocide and fanaticism quite as much as it is the narrative of Dante, Goethe and Chateaubriand, and this grimmer subtext is not wholly separable from its cultural splendours. The European humanist tradition has time and again served the cause of human emancipation; but when they are used to define an exclusivist identity, these mighty works of the spirit become the enemy of civilized values. Nor is Heaney wise to give the impression that moral culture stops at St Petersburg – though what does stop at St Petersburg, according to George Steiner, is coffee houses:

> Our Europe is still to an astonishing degree, after all the crises and changes, that Christian Roman Empire . . . if you draw a line from Porto in western Portugal to Leningrad, but certainly *not* Moscow, you can go to something called a coffee-house, with newspapers from all over Europe, you can play chess, play dominoes, you can sit all day for the price of a cup of coffee or a glass of wine, talk, read, work. Moscow, which is the beginning of Asia, has never had a coffee-house.[10]

As one savours one's coffee in St Petersburg, it is as well to spare a thought for those in the Great Asian Beyond who, bereft of both caffeine and dominoes, are sinking slowly into barbarism.

To cement the bonds of political unity, however, culture in the aesthetic sense is woefully inadequate. There was always something mildly risible about the idea that humanity might be saved by studying Shakespeare. To become a truly popular force, such elitist culture really needs to take the religious road. What the West ideally requires is some version of culture which would win the life-and-death allegiance of the people, and the traditional name for this allegiance is, precisely, religion. No form of culture has proved more potent in linking transcendent values with popular practices, the spirituality of the elite with the devotion of the masses. Religion is not effective because it is otherworldly, but because it incarnates this otherworldliness in a practical form of life. It can thus provide a link between Culture and culture, absolute values and daily life.

Matthew Arnold was quick to see this, and offered Culture as a replacement for a Christianity which was failing in its ideological functions. But he was also quick to see that religion combined culture in the sense of all-round cultivation with culture in the sense of principled action. If the Christian gospel is a matter of 'sweet reasonableness', or 'Hellenism', it is equally a question of implacable duties, or 'Hebraism'. Two senses of culture – as harmonious development (Greek) and as zealous commitment (Judaic) – could thus be agreeably harmonized.[11] If Hebraism could offset Hellenism's fatal bent for bland universality, Hellenism could equally moderate Hebraism's tendency to blind particularism. Patrician empty-mindedness and plebeian fanaticism could thus be held equally at bay. Spontaneity of consciousness (Hellenism) and strictness of consciousness (Hebraism) must temper one another, the former retrieved from upper-class frivolity and the latter from middle-class narrow-mindedness. This would also provide an equipoise between culture as contemplation and culture as action. The former was no longer tolerable in a period of political crisis, but culture would also check that tendency to intemperate action which was part of that crisis.

It proved, however, a paper solution. For one thing, any effort to revive religion, even in Arnold's poetically diluted version of it, is steadily sabotaged by capitalist secularization. It is capitalism's own this-worldly activities, not the atheistic left, which brings religion into disrepute, as a secularized base undermines the very spiritual superstructure it requires for its own stability. For another thing, any attempt to link Culture to religion now risks confronting the religious fundamentalism of others with one's own brand of the product, thus abandoning the high liberal-humanist ground and ending up embarrassingly indistinguishable from one's opponents. Too much Hellenism will fail against the religious zealots, but too much Hebraism will merely mimic them. Religious fundamentalism, which is the creed of those abandoned by modernity, will inspire men and women to militant action in defence of their society, as a dose of Dante or Dostoevsky will not. The only problem in the West is that such bigotry flies in the face of the very liberal values it is supposed to be defending. Western civilization must accordingly refuse such sectarianism, even if its own political and economic policies help to engender it. It is true that advanced capitalist orders need to ward off alienation and anomie with *some* kind of collective symbolism and ritual, complete with group solidarity, virile competition, a pantheon of legendary heroes and a carnivalesque release of repressed energies. But this is provided by sport, which conveniently combines the aesthetic aspect of Culture with the corporate dimension of culture, becoming for its devotees both an artistic experience and a whole way of life. It is interesting to speculate what the political effects of a society without sport would be.

If Culture is thrown into disarray by culture as solidarity, it is equally threatened by postmodern or cosmopolitan culture. In one sense, high and postmodern culture have increasingly fused to provide the cultural 'dominant' of Western societies. There is now hardly any high culture which is not tightly framed by capitalist priorities – which means that there is no problem in staging *The Tempest* provided you have the sponsorship of Marine Insurance. In any case, postmodernism has progressively eroded the frontiers between minority art and its mass or popular counterparts. Postmodern culture may be anti-patrician, but its demotic disdain for elitism can sit easily enough with an endorsement of conservative values. Nothing, after all, is more relentlessly value-levelling than the commodity form, a form which is hardly out of favour in conservative-minded societies. Indeed the more culture is commercialized, the more this imposition of market discipline forces its producers into the conservative values of prudence, anti-innovation and a nervousness of being disruptive. The market is the best mechanism for ensuring that society is both highly liberated and deeply reactionary. Commercial culture thus upholds many of the values of the high culture it scorns as elitist. It is just that it can wrap these values in an alluringly anti-elitist package, as high culture cannot.

Identity culture, equally, can be crossed with postmodern or commercial culture, as in the case of gay consumerism. And high culture is itself being increasingly invaded by the cultures of identity, to produce a crisis within the academic humanities. If, however, high culture means not so much minority art as certain spiritual values, then postmodernism has been busy sapping away at the moral and metaphysical foundations of the Western world at precisely the moment when these foundations need to be at their firmest. The enormous irony of this is worth pausing to consider. The very free-market operations by which the West imposes its authority on the rest of the world help to breed, back home, an increasingly sceptical, relativist culture; and this then helps to erode the spiritual authority ('Culture') which is needed to lend those global operations some veil of legitimacy. High culture may find postmodern culture distasteful, but it has a hand in propping up the very social order which allows such culture to circulate. Meanwhile, those who are the victims of this market culture turn increasingly to forms of militant particularism. In a three-way interaction, culture as spirituality is eroded by culture as the commodity, to give birth to culture as identity.

On a global scale, the relevant conflict here is between culture as commodity and culture as identity. The high culture of Bach and Proust can hardly compete as a material force with the seductions of the culture industry, a religious icon or a national flag. In Freudian terms, culture as sublimation is hardly able to rival culture as libidinal gratification. It is also less psychologically rooted than identity politics, which can be driven by ferocious pathological drives as well as by emancipatory ones. Postmodernism, with its scorn for tradition, stable selfhood and group solidarities, is bracingly sceptical of such politics, even if it is mistaken to see nothing in tradition but the dead hand of history and nothing in solidarity but coercive consensus. This may be true of neo-fascism or the North Dakota Militiamen for Jesus, but it is scarcely true of the African National Congress. Postmodernism can find little theoretical basis for such distinctions, and is thus in danger of consigning the working-class movement to the ashcan of history along with Utah fundamentalists and Ulster loyalists.

At the close of the twentieth century, the West has stepped boldly forward as the champion of humanity as a whole. Culture, one might say, is now the custodian of cultures. The particular, in Hegelian jargon, has been raised to the universal – a move which at once strengthens and threatens to undercut it. For any particular needs another particular to bounce off against, a need which the Cold War fulfilled with marvellous convenience; and the more the West now rolls over any alternative to itself, the weaker sense of identity it is likely to end up with. Rosa Luxembourg envisaged imperialism as expanding to the point where it had no territories left to conquer and so began to implode upon itself; and while this was no doubt rather too dewy-eyed a view, it is true that a system without apparent limits is likely to undergo if not a crisis of profits, then at least one of identity. How can a system, any more than a word, universalize itself without disappearing? Postmodernism is what happens when the system inflates to a point where it seems to negate all its opposites, and so no longer seems a system at all. Totality, stretched far enough, flips over into a mere host of random particulars. But since, being random, no one of these particulars can be defined against any other, they all end up looking suspiciously alike, and difference, pushed to an extreme, comes oddly to resemble identity. The more vividly particularized the world becomes, the more drearily uniform it grows, rather like those postmodern cities which all manufacture themselves as uniquely different by much the same techniques. One might argue conversely that what is nowadays dividing the world are the very processes which are supposed to be unifying it. Globalizing forces, for example, are quite content to see potentially threatening power-blocs broken up into a number of smaller, weaker nations, and occasionally take a hand in this break-up themselves. What mediates between difference and identity is structure – the way differences are articulated into a significant pattern, as in a narrative. But if that sense of articulation fails, if there is no longer a system, then it becomes difficult to say whether we are living in a world in which everything is dramatically different or increasingly identical. In any case, there can be no specificity without some general notion to contrast it with; and if generality is banished in the name of the particular, then it is only to be expected that the particular should eventually disappear along with it.

The West, however, need not fear for its identity just yet, since universalizing its own culture involves defending it against barbaric outsiders, as well as crushing regimes which dare to challenge its sway. Western culture is potentially universal, which means that it does not oppose its own values to those of others, merely reminds them that its own values are fundamentally theirs too. It is not trying to foist an alien identity on others, simply recalling them to what they secretly are. But the politics which promote this universality are necessarily partisan, which lends the West quite enough identity for the moment. Even so, it is having to universalize itself at just the point when its culture is being debilitated from within by an unholy alliance of postmodern scepticism and militant particularism. Besides, once the

West has defined itself as the wronged Goliath who will bring low the bullying Davids, the gap between its civilized culture and its actual conduct becomes to loom embarrassingly large, which is one danger of all such cultural idealism. Though such ideals are indispensable, they will for the most part simply show you how miserably short of them you fall.

It is here that postmodernism wins itself some contrasting credibility. For postmodernism tells it like it is rather than like it ought to be, a realism which one needs quite as much as one needs idealism. It is just that the two are bound to be askew to each other. Postmodernism is sassy and streetwise as cultural idealism is not, but it pays an enormous price for this pragmatism. It is adept at kicking the foundations out from under other people's positions; but it cannot do this without kicking them out simultaneously from under itself, and though this move may seem of no great moment in Berkeley or Brighton, its global implications are rather less trivial. Such pragmatism leaves the West disarmed in the face of those fundamentalisms, both within and without, which are not too perturbed by other people's anti-metaphysical eagerness to scupper their own foundations. It leaves the West with no more than a culturalist apologia for its actions – 'this is just what we white Western bourgeois happen to do, take it or leave it' – which is not only philosophically feeble but shows up as absurdly inadequate in the light of the formidable global authority which this region of the world now actually claims for itself.

If your self-appointed brief is to instruct the rest of humankind in correct moral conduct, it is advisable to muster one or two rather more imposing-looking rationales for yourself than this. Any more robust sort of self-rationalization, however, in terms of the Will of God, the Destiny of the West or the White Man's Burden, is bound to ring rather hollow in the pragmatic, disenchanted, distinctly unmetaphysical climate of advanced capitalism. It is the system itself which has ruled these rationales out of order, much as it might profit from them. Capitalism is naturally anti-foundational, melting all that is solid into air, and this provokes its fundamentalist reactions within the West as well as beyond it. Divided between Evangelism and emancipation, *Forrest Gump* and *Pulp Fiction*, Western culture is thus further weakened in its confrontation with the world beyond. The term 'sub-culture' is among other things an unconscious way of disavowing this disunity, implying as it does a contrast with some readily identifiable supra-culture. But most modern societies are in fact a cluster of intersecting sub-cultures, and it is becoming harder to say from what normative cultural world a particular sub-culture deviates. If the nose-ringed and purple-haired constitute a sub-culture, so in more and more places do households where all the children are the joint off-spring of the resident parents.

Anti-foundationalism reflects a hedonist, pluralist, open-ended culture which is genuinely more tolerant than its elders, but which can also yield real market benefits. In the end, however, this moral climate helps to line your coffers only at the risk of eroding the authority which guarantees your right to do so. Advanced capitalism is forced to sacrifice the well-foundedness of the self to its freedom, as though what now thwarted that freedom was nothing less than the identity which enjoyed it. This was not a choice which a more classical phase of the same system felt obliged to contemplate. But there is, needless to say, more to anti-foundational thought than some dark marketeering conspiracy. It can also provide a precious critique of the more sinister aspects of culture as earth and *ethos*. It is dangerous to assume that one's collective identity has cosmic backing, even if there are cultures of solidarity which are also wary of such notions. Most feminism would be one case in point. Even so, there is an important difference between dispensing with essences and foundations because who you are is no longer such a burning issue, and dispensing with them when you need a fairly secure sense of who you are just in order to become what you want to be. If you do not know who you are in the West, postmodernism is on hand to tell you not to worry; if you do not know who you are in less well-heeled areas of the globe, you may need to create the conditions in which it becomes possible to find out. One traditional name for this inquiry has been revolutionary nationalism, which is not at all to the taste of postmodern theory. It represents, so to speak, particularity without hybridity, rather as cosmopolitanism might be described as the converse. There are some, in short, who can buy their anti-foundationalism on the cheap, just as there are some who, having worked their way through the agenda of modernity, can afford to be rather more sardonic about it than those who have not.

One ends up in any case with a world in which some are all too sure of who they are while others are too little so – two conditions which are by no means unrelated. In fact postmodern culture typically includes both identity politics and the cult of the decentred subject. There are, to be sure, other forms of identity politics, all the way from family values and Zionism to communitarianism and Islam, for which postmodernism may be the devil incarnate. But even here we should note some affinities. Both postmodern culture and culture as identity tend to conflate the cultural and the political. They are also alike in their particularist suspicion of high culture's universalist claims. Postmodernism is not universalist but cosmopolitan, which is quite a different matter. The global space of postmodernism is hybrid, whereas the space of universalism is unitary. The universal is compatible with the national – universal culture, for example, sees itself as a gallery of the finest works of national cultures – whereas cosmopolitan culture transgresses national boundaries as surely as do money and transnational corporations.

For both postmodern culture and identity culture, there is something more than artworks – 'life-style' in the case of postmodernism, forms of life for culture as identity. And when it comes to the post-colonial world, there are other connections too. A cultural relativism hatched in the postmodern West, and reflecting its own crisis of identity, can be exported to post-colonial nations in ways which underpin the most dogmatic forms of separatism and supremacism. As Meera Nanda points out, the postmodern doctrine that truth is culture-bound can end up 'providing theoretical grounds for, and a progressive gloss on, the fast growing anti-modernist, nativist, and cultural/religious revivalist movements in many parts of what used to be called the third world'.[12] What may seem the last word in epistemological radicalism in Paris can end up justifying autocracy elsewhere. In a curious reversal, cultural relativism can come to ratify the most virulent forms of cultural absolutism. In its charitable view that all cultural worlds are as good as each other, it provides a rationale by which any one of them may be absolutized. A similar incongruity can be observed in Northern Ireland, where the more astute Ulster Unionists have learnt to speak the language of multiculturalism.

One reason why postmodernism looks persuasive is that it promises to avoid the worst features of both Culture and culture, while preserving their more attractive qualities. If it shares the cosmopolitanism of high culture, it rejects its elitism; if it has the populism of culture as form of life, it has no patience with its organicist nostalgia. Like high culture, postmodernism is much taken with the aesthetic, though more as style and pleasure than canonical artefact; but it is a kind of 'anthropological' culture too, including clubs, fashion-houses, architecture and shopping malls as well as texts and videos. Like culture as way of life, it celebrates the particular, though a particular which is provisional rather than rooted, hybrid rather than whole. However, since postmodernism affirms the demotic and vernacular wherever on the globe it happens to find them, it combines its particularism with a certain cavalier indifference to place. Its demotic sympathies spring more from a scepticism of hierarchies than, as with culture as solidarity, from a commitment to the dispossessed. Its egalitarianism is as much a product of the commodity as a resistance to it.

Much the same could be said of the difference between cosmopolitanism and internationalism. Universalism belongs to high culture, cosmopolitanism to the culture of global capitalism, while internationalism is a form of political resistance to that world. The socialist slogan 'Workers of the world, unite!' itself unites internationalism and solidarity, two doctrines that are today increasingly dissevered. Internationalism is now a feature of the capitalist system itself, while the solidarities which oppose it are mostly local. If it is now the uprooted migrant of post-colonialism who has no homeland, it was once the international labour movement. And it was *Kultur*, the cultural ideology which reached its nadir in the Third Reich, which denounced that internationalism as decadence, Jewishness, rootlessness, conspiracy.

But though the working-class movement acknowledged no homeland, it was inevitably situated within one; and this allowed it a rather different conception of the relationship between the particular and the universal. Universal community was the goal, and internationalism the means; but since workers are always tied to the spot, in contrast to the perpetual mobility of capital, both ends and means could be attained only through the local and specific.

The socialist movement, in short, conjoined the particular and the universal rather as the nation-state had tried to do, but in a way which involved striving to bring that state low. For socialist thought, capitalism, the first truly global mode of production, has laid down some of the conditions for a more positive kind of universality. But for Marx at least, that universality had to be realized at the level of individual specificity. Communism would be a relation between the free, fully developed individuals engendered by liberal bourgeois society, not some nostalgic regression to the pre-bourgeois epoch. If universality could be constructed, it could only be in and through sensuous particularity, in contrast to a 'bad' Enlightenment universality which tried to by-pass it. If postmodernism is a universalized particularism, the vision of socialism is of a particularized universalism. Capitalist universalism had done its job by pitching together a host of different cultures, indifferently overriding the distinctions between them. It now remained for socialism to seize advantage of this fact by building a universal culture on these very differences. What was a fact for capitalism would become thus a value for socialism. Marx is as hostile to the *abstraction* of universality from difference as he is to the divorce of the abstract citizen from the concrete individual, or of the abstraction of exchange-value from the sensuous specificity of use-value.

Socialist internationalism no longer exists in any significant form. But this is one of several reasons why culture is caught in a cleft stick between a flawed universalism and an equally blemished particularism. For socialist thought, universality is inherent in the local, not an alternative to it. What is fought for in Bradford is relevant to those fighting in Bangkok, though the two struggles will take different forms. Culture as universal value, and culture as a specific life-form, are not necessarily antagonists. This is sometimes forgotten by those who would excuse the illiberalism of the oppressed on the grounds of their political circumstances. There is indeed some grounds for excuse here; but plenty of the oppressed, not least in the form of socialist working men and women, have been globally minded rather than ghetto-minded because of their beliefs, not in spite of them. Those beliefs have led them to sympathize with people of very different creeds and cultures, in contrast with those of the dispossessed for whom such men and women are infidels to be purged. Those Western liberals who defend this intolerance because in the circumstances it is only to be expected are thus both patronizing and ignorant of socialist traditions.

In any case, it is not a choice between being a citizen of the world and a member of one's local parish, if only because we are both of these for different purposes on different occasions. Both culture as civility and culture as identity are dogmatic in this respect, insisting as they do that only the synoptic view, or only a specific *prise de position*, can be valid. As such, they are merely the inverse of one another. The truth is that we live increasingly in divided and distinguished worlds, and have still to come to terms with the fact. There is no 'given' size of society, whether it is the neighbourhood streets of the communitarian, the homeland of the nativist, the planetary space of the transnational corporations or the international solidarity of the socialist. All such spaces are pliable and interwoven, and almost everyone now maintains relations to a range of them simultaneously. We need, as Raymond Williams comments, 'to explore new forms of *variable* societies, in which over the whole range of social purposes different *sizes* of society are defined for different kinds of issue and decision'.[13] It is hardly a surprising statement from one who described himself as a Welsh European, and who never tired of insisting that the nation-state was both too cumbersome and too inconsiderable for any politics which really mattered.

There is, then, a geopolitical hybridity as well as a cultural or ethnic one, and to grasp this can lead us beyond both Culture and culture. If cultures can be claustrophobic, it may be because their members lack the means to participate in wider political groupings. The intensity of our local attachments springs to some extent from a more widespread alienation. But it is a combination of lived attachments, some local, some not, which we most need to negotiate. How we 'live' our relations to a supranational order like the EU is a political rather than cultural affair, at least for the moment; but this relationship overlaps with more local, cultural allegiances, as well as with ethical commitments which are properly universal. There is no need to imagine that each of these orders should smoothly mediate the others, or that they should always be ranked in a particular order. Francis Mulhern reminds us that there can be no simple contrast between 'identity', 'community' and the 'universal' – not only because identity is itself a universal necessity of human existence, but because we are all a complex of such identities.

Communities, Mulhern argues, are 'not *places* but *practices* of collective identification whose variable order largely defines the culture of any actual social formation'.[14] As such, they can be as much universal as local, and to limit the notion to the latter is to fetishize it. One can speak of 'abstract communities', or see the nation as a 'community of known strangers'.[15] The relations between culture and politics are similarly variable, depending on the context. There should be no Enlightenment assumption that politics always has the edge over culture, or – as with so much culturalist thought – that it is enough simply to invert this order of priorities. There can no longer, in short, be that dream of identity between the rational and the affective, the civic and the cultural, which the hyphen in 'nation-state' sought to secure. Indeed nationalism, which helped to forge that hyphen, might nowadays help to dislodge it, as a democratic devolution of power within a larger international community.

There are other ways, however, in which radical politics challenges both the flawed universality of Culture and the blemished particularism of culture. It does so, for example, in its refusal to see totality and partisanship as simple opposites. For Culture, totality is the disinterested viewpoint of those who in Arnoldian spirit see life steadily and see it whole. The only valid view, in brief, is the view from nowhere. Views from somewhere, such as those of specific cultures, are inevitably partial and distorting. Radicals, by contrast, recognize no such choice between sectoral interests and global impartiality, as women or ethnic minorities or the working-class movement come to see in the promotion of their own self-interested goals the possibility of a more general emancipation. Particular social groups can now be the bearers of common interests in their very partisanship. Society is to be totalized not from a privileged point above it, but from a subordinate point within it. The logic of an entire situation can be deciphered only by those at a specific angle to it, since it is they who most need this knowledge for the ends of emancipation. They are, as we say, in a position to know, a homely phrase which denies that positionality is necessarily at odds with truth.

Globally speaking, it does not look as though the West is particularly well placed to win the culture wars. At least that might well be one's conclusion were it not for the fact that culture as civility has an enormous armed force behind it. If high culture is too rarefied to be an effective political force, much postmodern culture is too brittle, rootless and depoliticized. Neither shows up especially well when compared to Islam, for which culture is historically rooted and inescapably political. It is also a form of life for which considerable numbers of people are prepared to die, which may not be a wise policy, but which is more than can be said for Mozart or Madonna. The wonders of satellite communications do not shape up well against sacred scripture. Moreover, the more a two-dimensional postmodern culture is exported to the post-colonial world, the more, by reaction, it can fan the flames of cultural particularism there.

Postmodernism, at least in its more theoretical aspects, may be a valuable way for the West to deflate its own overweening identity. But when it arrives in the post-colonial world in the shape of a slick consumerism, it can pitch traditional identities and communities there into much less creative forms of crisis. Such crisis has far more to do with homelessness, migration and unemployment than it has to do with *jouissance*, and can feed a fundamentalism which is the very last thing an endlessly open-minded postmodernism is out to foster. Much the same happens in fundamentalist enclaves within the West itself.

By a curious dialectic, then, fundamentalism and anti-foundationalism are by no means the polar opposites they would appear. The latter may end up unwittingly in the service of the former. The final triumph of capitalism – to see its own culture penetrate to the most inconspicuous corners of the globe – may also prove exceptionally dangerous for it.

The strife between high culture, culture as identity and postmodern culture is not a matter of the cosmopolitan versus the local, since all three combine these in different ways. High culture may be cosmopolitan, but it is also usually nation-based; identity cultures may be localized, but they may also be as international as feminism or Islam. And postmodern culture, as we have seen, is a kind of universalized particularism. Nor is the quarrel between these types of culture primarily one between 'high' and 'low', since so-called high culture itself cuts increasingly across this division, and the culture of identity has its sacred artefacts as well as its popular icons. Postmodernism, similarly, spans the demotic and the esoteric, the streetwise and the avant-garde. Nor is the difference between these formations one of geographical distribution. In Asia as well as in North America you can find high culture, whether local or cosmopolitan, in the universities and among the intelligentsia, postmodernism in the same places too but also in the discos and shopping malls, while culture as identity flourishes in sub-cultures, populist political parties and perhaps among the dispossessed.

Even so, the political conflict between Culture and culture is increasingly a geopolitical one as well. The most important contentions between high and popular culture are not between Stravinsky and soap opera, but between Western civility and all that it squares up to elsewhere. What it confronts elsewhere is culture – but culture as a brew of nationalism, tradition, religion, ethnicity and popular sentiment which far from qualifying as cultivation in the eyes of the West, ranks as its very opposite. And these enemies can also be found within the gates. Those for whom culture is the reverse of militancy face off against those for whom culture and militancy are inseparable. As it rides roughshod over local communities and traditional sentiments,

Western society leaves a culture of smouldering *ressentiment* in its wake. The more a false universalism slights specific identities, the more inflexibly those identities are asserted. Each position thus steadily paints the other into a corner. Since Culture reduces the revolutionary William Blake to a timeless human utterance, it is all the easier for culture as identity to write him off as a Dead White Male, thus perversely depriving itself of some precious political resources.

In all of this, it is hard to see what is 'modern' and what is not. 'Globalization' is the *dernier cri*, but it could just as well be seen as the latest phase of a mode of production which has long outstayed its welcome. The West is modern, yet the religion and high culture it calls upon to legitimate itself are traditionalist. It derives its official moral code from a 'Third World' society, first-century Palestine. Some forms of identity politics – feminism, for example – are a product of modernity, while others (communitarianism, religious fundamentalism) are a last-ditch resistance to it. Even postmodernism, which for some of its acolytes is not only the latest game in town but positively the last, can as plausibly be seen as the jaded culture of a late bourgeois world.

Alternatively, one could see it as a fairly traditional creed. In some ways, it is just the latest offensive of the nominalist camp which waged war in the Middle Ages against the ontological realists. Indeed Frank Farrell has persuasively argued that both modernism and postmodernism are really of late medieval origin.[16] Medieval theologians were divided between those for whom the world was thin and indeterminate, and those for whom it was thick and determinate, the stake to play for here being the freedom of God. If the world is rich with inherent meaning, then God's liberty to do what he likes with it, and hence his omnipotence, would seem drastically constrained. If reality is both arbitrary and of low definition, however, then it puts up no resistance to the divine will and God's absolute freedom would seem secured. Either you hold that God acts with respect for the intrinsic properties of his world, or that the world has no properties other than those with which he gratuitously imbues it. It is a version of the hoary old moral question of whether God wills something because it is good, or whether it is good because he wills it. The Catholic tradition adheres by and large to the former, 'realist' case, while the latter, 'constructivist' position will pass on into Protestantism.

The modern, Protestant-individualist self thus becomes a kind of surrogate deity, imbuing with arbitrary meaning a world stripped of 'thick' significances and sensuous properties. Rationalism can find only a thin, notional, mathematical kind of determinacy in the world, which plunders it of its material wealth but leaves it as so much raw material for the subject's ceaseless productivity. This subject is now the sole source of meaning and value, and in its absolute, God-like freedom brooks no constraint. The only limits placed upon it are those of the determinate objects it creates, which can always slip from its sovereign control and return to plague it. Even this problem, however, can be wished away, as in Fichte's hubristic doctrine – surely the ultimate bourgeois fantasy – that the subject posits its own constraints simply in order to realize its freedom in the triumphant act of transcending them. All determination thus becomes self-determination. What is real is only what I have mixed with my labour, or what I can personally authenticate. The world for this strenuous Protestant humanism has no significance in itself: it is a dark, fearful, inhospitable place where we can never feel at home. It is thus an essentially tragic philosophy, as opposed to that cosmic at-homeness, that conviction of all being ultimately well, which is the essence of comedy.

We have seen that with Arnold and others, Culture becomes a kind of displaced religion; but this may also be true, more surprisingly, of the secularized culture of modern and postmodern life. If postmodernity is really a belated form of Protestantism, then this aligns it with modernity rather than puts it at odds with it. Where the two cultures diverge, however, is in their contrasting attitudes to emancipation. For the postmodernists, this notion belongs to a discredited modernity, with its Whiggish grand narratives. But if postmodernity is out ahead of modernity, there is also a sense in which it trails behind. For modernity is still an aspiration for many of the world's nations whose modernizing project has been held back by colonialism – which is to say, by the modernizing project of the West. If they cannot always afford to be postmodern, it is partly because the West can. In the twentieth century, then, much – if by no means all – of the emancipatory project of modernity has passed beyond the West's frontiers, to peoples claiming their independence of colonial rule.

A good deal of post-colonial theory – that sector of it which acts, so to speak, as the State Department or Foreign Office of Western postmodernism, dealing with overseas affairs – is convinced that this heroic moment of modernity is as outdated in the post-colonial world as it is in the post-colonialist one. This is why we now have talk of hybridity, ethnicity and plurality, rather than of freedom, justice and emancipation. But this is to synchronize the histories of the colonialist and colonial worlds in a dangerously misleading way. The truth is that for post-colonial nations whose destinies are still determined by the vicissitudes of Western capital, the project of emancipation remains as relevant as ever, however much the political and economic forms of their clientship may have changed. It is just that the West plays a major role in blocking that project for others by believing that it has left it behind itself. To consign modernity to the past is thus to help obstruct the future. If some, in this curious time-warping, must run hard to catch up with modernity, it is partly because others see themselves as out in front of it. Quite who is 'modern' here is then notably hard to say.

If capitalism is by no means as up-to-date as it looks, neither are some forms of identity culture as archaic as they seem. We are becoming accustomed these days to the fact that plenty of venerable-looking traditions are of embarrassingly recent vintage, and that a good many insights which supposedly sprang up with Habermas in fact go back to Heraclitus. It is true that nationalism, perhaps the most tenacious of all identity cultures, is often *atavistic*, but that is a different matter. Atavism aside, nationalism is a thoroughly modern invention, a good deal more recent than Shakespeare, though Shakespeare belongs to the cultural repertoire of a 'modern' West and nationalism, by and large, to the lexicon of a 'backward' world. You can see the collective subject of nationalism as a reversion to tribalism, but you can see it just as well as prefiguring a post-individualist world. If nationalism turns its gaze to a (usually fictitious) past, it is largely to press forward to an imagined future. This particular time-warping, which reinvents the past as a way of laying claim to the future, has been responsible in our time for some brave experiments in popular democracy, as well as for an appalling amount of bigotry and butchery. Identity politics is one of the most uselessly amorphous of all political categories, including as it does those who wish to liberate themselves from tribal patriarchs along with those who wish to exterminate them. But this kind of politics can hardly be adequately addressed by a postmodernism which is busy liquidating both past and future in the name of an eternal present. Nor can it be properly addressed by a Culture which considers itself timeless in a rather different sense of the term. If Culture cannot save us, it is because it does not really think of itself as historical at all, and so has no title to intervene in sublunary affairs.

Culture promises to bulk large in the coming decades, but this, which would have been music to Matthew Arnold's ears, is by no means to be unequivocally welcomed. If culture in our time has become a medium of affirmation, it has also discovered new forms of dominion. But we should remember that the culture wars are finally four-way rather than three-way. There is also the culture of opposition, which has produced some distinguished work in the twentieth century. Oppositional culture is not necessarily a category in itself; on the contrary, it can be produced by high, postmodern and identity culture, or by various permutations of all three. It has known several major blossomings in the twentieth century, in the Russian avant garde, in Weimar and in the counterculture of the 1960s, but has withered each time as the political forces which underpinned it were defeated. It has learnt enough from this experience to know that the success or failure of radical culture is determined in the end by one fact alone: the fortunes of a broader political movement.

4

Culture and Nature

It is evidently quite possible to cut off one's own hand without feeling pain. People whose hand has become trapped in machinery have sometimes amputated it painlessly, distracted as they were by the need to disentangle themselves. Political protestors have also been known to set themselves on fire without feeling a thing, their pain blocked out by the intensity of their passion. Someone may smack a child quite lightly for some offence and he will cry, but you may smack him much harder in the course of a game only to evoke a delighted laugh. On the other hand, if you smack a child really hard in jest, he is quite likely to cry even so. Meanings can mould physical responses, but they are constrained by them too. The adrenal glands of the poor are often larger than those of the rich, since the poor suffer more stress, but poverty is not able to create adrenal glands where none exist. Such is the dialectic of nature and culture.

People who set themselves on fire may feel no pain, but if they burn themselves badly enough they will perish even so. In this sense, nature has the final victory over culture, customarily known as death. Culturally speaking, death is almost limitlessly interpretable, as martyrdom, ritual sacrifice, blessed release from agony, joyous freedom for one's long-suffering kinsfolk, natural biological end, union with the cosmos, symbol of ultimate futility and the like. But we still die, however we make sense of it. Death is the limit of discourse, not a product of it. It is part of nature, which in Kate Soper's words means 'those material structures and processes that are independent of human activity (in the sense that they are not a humanly created product), and whose forces and causal powers are the necessary condition of every human practice'.[1] The kind of hubris which denies this, which one might dub the California syndrome, is to be expected from a triumphalist technocracy which can vanquish everything but mortality. Hence, no doubt, the middle-class American obsession with the body, which crops up in almost all of its fashionable preoccupations: cancer, dieting, smoking, sport, hygiene, fitness, mugging, sexuality, child abuse. Literary studies whose titles do not contain the word 'body' are looked on with disfavour these days by US publishing houses. Perhaps this is because a pragmatist society believes in the end only in what it can touch and handle.

But the sheer givenness of the body, slim, pierce, silicone or tattoo it as one might, is also a scandal to the American dream of self-creation. There is more than a touch of this in the postmodern insistence that the body is a cultural construct, as much clay in the hands of the imaginative interpreter as it is stuff to be pummelled in the hands of the masseur. In circles which are more and more keen on the organic, the word 'natural' evokes a curious antipathy. The American philosopher Richard Rorty writes that 'the only lesson of either history or anthropology is our extraordinary malleability. We are coming to think of ourselves as the flexible, protean, self-shaping animal rather than as the rational animal or the cruel animal'.[2] One wonders whether the 'we' includes those beyond the euphorically self-shaping United States whose history has been most remarkable for its *lack* of flexibility – for being little more than a monotonous biological round of need, scarcity and political oppression, to which the mercurial West might well have contributed. This, in fact, has been the typical experience of by far the majority of human beings in history, and remains so today. Sheer dull persistence has characterized the human narrative considerably more than giddying re-creation, however things might look from the University of Virginia. Mind-numbing repetition has been at least as central to the story as the protean reinventions of the US fashion industry.

The American fetish of the body is a curious mixture of hedonism and puritanism – unsurprisingly, no doubt, since hedonism is the puritan's outraged idea of enjoyment. It is thus that one can find supermarkets in the United States with signs on the doors reading 'No smoking within 25 yards of this store', or diet-conscious regions in which stout Santa Clauses are now out of favour. The American middle-class terror of smoking is in one sense eminently rational, since smoking can be lethal; but smoke also signifies the impalpable influence by which one body invades and contaminates another, in a society which values its somatic space and unlike Beijing has more than enough of it to spare. An American will murmur 'Excuse me' if she approaches within five yards of you. The pathological US fear of smoking is as much a fear of extra-terrestrials as it is of lung cancer. Like the loathsome creatures of *Alien*, smoke and cancer are those dreadful bits of otherness which manage somehow to insinuate themselves at the core of one's being. So indeed are food and drink, which middle-class America now approaches in fear and trembling. Which bits of these perilous substances to shovel inside yourself has now become a national neurosis. Sleep, too, is a surrender of the body to uncontrollable forces, which may be one reason (the profit motive is no doubt another) why Americans seem unable to stay in bed. Hillary Clinton recently had a *pre-dawn* breakfast with her advisors.

Perhaps this is why American cultural studies are so fascinated by the carnivalesque, whose sprawling, licentious body represents everything that the buttoned-down puritan body is not. And if the body needs to be purged of its impurities, so does language, in that fetishism of discourse known as political correctness. A man in Standish, Michigan recently fell into a river and almost drowned. On being rescued he was arrested for cursing in front of women and children, an offence which carries a maximum penalty of ninety days in gaol. The toneless, tight-lipped, contrivedly artless language favoured by American creative writing courses reflects a puritan suspicion of style, which is equivalent to effeteness. It was Bill Clinton's equivocations, as much as his penchant for oral sex, which condemned him as a fancy boy in the eyes of plain-speaking Republicans. Perhaps this accounts for something of the success of post-structuralist ambiguity in the United States, as a reaction to a society where straight talking is next to Godliness. No solemn historical event in the United States is complete without a home-spun metaphor drawn from baseball. A suspicion of form as falsehood, inherited from an earlier phase of bourgeois society, is still widespread in a nation which is in thrall to the simulacrum yet pays scant heed to style. There is little middle ground in American discourse between the formal and the folksy, between the baroque jargon of academia and the cut-the-crap raciness of common speech. In a Jamesian distinction, Europe may be *fine*, all style and wit and brio, but America is *good*, and must be prepared to pay the unlovely price of such virtuousness.

This affects public discourse too, which in the United States remains earnestly Victorian, full of bland, high-minded pieties: 'Proudly serving America's families since 1973'; 'Celebrating the joy of kids growing through interaction' (a cereal advertisement); 'A very fine American of probity and integrity'. It is an upbeat, superlative idiom, as befits a society where gloom and negativity are regarded as ideologically subversive. The sentimental, moralistic rhetoric of an earlier stage of capitalist production, full of wide-eyed zest and relentless can-do-ery, has survived into the cynically consumerist present. The nation is in the grip of a remorseless voluntarism, which rages against material constraint and insists with all the idealist fantasizing of a Fichte that you can crack it if you try. 'I am stronger than a 250 pound child molester', lies a child on a public poster. 'I don't like to hear the word "can't"', protests a business executive. It is not a society hospitable to failure or suffering. 'I hope there ain't anyone sick in here', bawls an entertainer visiting a hospital, as though illness were anti-American. Children's television is an orgy of grinning and beaming, a heavily didactic medium pedalling a warped version of the world as relentlessly bright. In notably bad taste, one is even expected to sing the praises of one's own children. American politicians still use the high-toned language of divinity to justify their shady doings, in ways which would make the French crumple with derisive laughter and the English stare embarrassedly at their shoes. Emotion must be theatricalized to be real. Whatever is felt is to be instantly externalized, in a culture unused to reticence or obliquity. And while public rhetoric grows inflated, private speech crumbles almost to silence. A statement like 'He rejected my proposal, and even though I kept insisting he was adamant in his refusal', becomes in some youthful American-English 'Like he was all "uh-uh" and I was like kinda "hey!" but he was like "no way" or whatever'.

If European determinism springs from being suffocated by history, American voluntarism comes from stifling for lack of it. You may thus reinvent yourself whenever you want, an agreeable fantasy which Richard Rorty has raised to the dignity of a philosophy. The Chief Justice in the impeachment hearings over President Clinton processed into the Senate wearing a regulation black robe to which he had added a few gold bands, inspired by a recent performance of Gilbert and Sullivan's *Iolanthe*. American Mormons, striving to reconcile the age of the universe with their belief that God fashioned it fairly recently, claim that God created the world to look older than it is. The cosmos, in the language of the antiques trade, is 'distressed', and much the same goes for some American traditions. Indeed Mormonism itself is among other things a crew-cutted reaction to the scandal that Jesus Christ was a non-American, pre-modern Semite. And if the United States is relatively unconstrained by history, it is equally remote from geography, a subject in which it is notoriously unproficient. As one of the most parochial societies in the world, it is marooned from anywhere but Canada (too much the same) and Latin America (too fearfully different), with astonishingly little sense of how it is seen from the outside. If people of truly surreal fatness complacently patrol its streets, it is partly because they have no idea that this is not happening everywhere else. Americans use the word 'America' much more frequently than Danes use the word 'Denmark' or Malaysians 'Malaysia'. No doubt this is what happens when your view of other countries is for the most part through a camera lens or from a bomber.

Much postmodern 'culturalism' – the doctrine that everything in human affairs is a matter of culture – becomes intelligible once one returns it to this context. The culturalists, in short, must themselves be culturalized, and the postmodern insistence on historicizing turned on postmodern theory itself. For culturalism, which joins biologism, economism, essentialism and the like as one of the great contemporary reductionisms, there is no question of a dialectic between Nature and culture, since Nature is cultural in any case. It is not clear what it means to claim that, say, bleeding or Mont Blanc are cultural. It is true that the *concepts* of bleeding and Mont Blanc, with all their rich freight of implications, are cultural; but this is a mere tautology, since what else could a concept be? However could anyone imagine that it was not? As the Italian philosopher Sebastiano Timpanaro remarks, 'To maintain that, since the "biological" is always presented to us as mediated by the "social", the "biological" is nothing and the "social" is everything, would . . . be idealist sophistry'.[3]

Kate Soper has shown in *What Is Nature?* the logical incoherence of the culturalist case, which just to make its point is forced to posit the existence of the very realities it denies. For this 'metaphysical anti-naturalism', nature, sex and the body are wholly the products of convention – in which case it is hard to know how one is supposed to judge, for example, that one sexual regime is more emancipated than another.[4] In any case, why is everything reducible to culture, rather than to some other thing? And how do we establish this momentous truth? By cultural means, one assumes; but is this not rather like claiming that everything boils down to religion, and that we know this because the law of God tells us so?

There are other well-aired problems with such cultural relativism. Is the belief that everything is culturally relative itself relative to a cultural framework? If it is, then there is no need to accept it as gospel truth; if it is not, then it undercuts its own claim. And does the proposition not seem to aspire to a universal validity which it also disowns? Cultural relativists dislike talk of universals, but such talk is an integral part of many cultural set-ups, and not just of the West. This is one of several senses in which the local and the universal are by no means polar opposites, whatever a postmodernism supposedly hostile to binary oppositions may believe. If talk of universals functions fruitfully enough within these local set-ups, enriching the language and enforcing some productive distinctions, why censor it? Pragmatism, a creed which many cultural relativists promote, would seem to yield no grounds on which to do so. Though if pragmatism judges the truth of theories by what one can get out of them, cultural relativism would seem an odd doctrine for it to espouse, since it appears to make no practical difference. Indeed, as Wittgenstein might say, it cancels all the way through and leaves everything exactly as it was. Some cultural relativists are less pragmatists than coherentists, holding that a belief is true if it coheres with the rest of our beliefs. But to judge this would seem to require just the kind of realist epistemology which coherentism rejects. How exactly do we ascertain that our beliefs fit together? Anyway, if all cultures are relative, then all of them are ethnocentric – in which case no special stigma attaches to the West in this regard.

There is a well-entrenched postmodern doctrine that the natural is no more than an insidious naturalization of culture. It is difficult to see quite how this applies either to bleeding or to Mont Blanc, but the claim is nonetheless frequently made. The natural, a word which must nowadays be compulsively draped in scare quotes, is simply the cultural frozen, arrested, consecrated, dehistoricized, converted into spontaneous common sense or taken-for-granted truth. It is true that a good deal of culture is like this; but not all culture mistakes itself as eternal and unalterable, a fact which may render it all the more politically recalcitrant. Not all centre-left liberal democrats imagine that their creed was vigorously flourishing at the time of Nebuchadnezzar. From Edmund Burke to Michael Oakshott, historicism, not metaphysical stasis, has been one of the dominant ideologies of European conservatism for the last two centuries. And some cultural prejudices really do seem at least as tenacious as ivy or barnacles. It is easier to root out weeds than it is sexism. To transform a whole culture would be a good deal more laborious than damming a river or razing a mountain. In this sense at least, nature is much more tractable stuff than culture. In any case, people do not always stoically endure what they regard as natural. Typhoid is natural, but we spend a lot of energy trying to eradicate it.

It is curious to view nature in these piously Wordsworthian terms as timeless, inevitable and mutely enduring, in an epoch where it is all too flagrantly pliable material. In fact the pejorative postmodern use of 'natural' is interestingly at odds with the postmodern ecological acknowledgement of nature's sickening fragility. Many cultural phenomena have proved more obdurately persistent than a rainforest. And the sovereign theory of nature in our time has been one of process, struggle, unending variation. It is the professional apologists for culture, not the explorers of nature, who insist on caricaturing nature as inert and immobile, rather as it is only those in the humanities who insist on retaining the old-fashioned image of science as positivist, disinterested, reductionist and the rest, if only for the self-righteous delight of knocking it down. The humanities have always despised the natural sciences; it is just that whereas this antipathy once took the form of regarding scientists as unspeakable yokels with fluff in their ears and leather patches on their jacket elbows, it nowadays assumes the guise of a suspicion of transcendent knowledge. The only drawback with this anti-scientific attitude is that it has been shared by most interesting philosophers of science for rather a long time.

Culturalism is an understandable overreaction to a naturalism which, from Thomas Hobbes to Jeremy Bentham, saw humanity in virulently anti-cultural terms as a mere assemblage of fixed bodily appetites. This was also a hedonistic creed, for which pain and pleasure were paramount – ironically, since a rather different cult of pleasure crops up in culturalism. Culturalism, however, is not only a suspiciously self-serving creed for cultural intellectuals, but in some ways an inconsistent one, since it tends to decry the natural while reproducing it. If culture really does go all the way down, then it seems to play just the same role as nature, and feels just as natural to us. This, at least, is true of any *particular* culture, though the point of culturalism is to insist that all actual cultures are also in a sense arbitrary. I have to be *some* kind of cultural being, but not any specific kind of cultural being. So there is something inescapably ironic about my being Armenian, since I might always have been from Arkansas. But then I should not have been who I am, so being Armenian feels perfectly natural to me after all, and the fact that I might have been from Arkansas is neither here nor there.

To claim that we are entirely cultural creatures absolutizes culture with one hand while relativizing the world with the other. It is rather like asserting that flux is the foundation of the universe. If culture really is wall-to-wall, constitutive of my very selfhood, then it is hard for me to imagine not being the cultural being I am, which is just what a knowledge of the relativity of my culture invites me to do. Indeed it is just what culture in another sense – the creative imagination – insists that I do. How can one be both cultured and cultured, inexorably shaped by a way of life yet brimming with imaginative empathy for other such life-worlds? It seems that I have somehow to sit loose to the very difference which defines me, hardly the most comfortable of postures to maintain.

Culturalists divide between those like Richard Rorty who rather cerebrally promote such an ironic posture, and those like the Stanley Fish of *Doing What Comes Naturally* who insist, more alarmingly but rather more plausibly, that if my culture goes all the way down then it is right and inevitable for me to 'naturalize' it as absolute. Any understanding of another culture will then be just a move within my own. Either we are prisoners of our culture, or we can transcend it only by cultivating an ironic habit of mind. And the latter is a privilege confined to the civilized few. Indeed social life would cease to function if it became too widespread. Rorty's distinction between irony and popular belief is just another version of Althusser's dichotomy of theory and ideology.

What both cases fail to see is that it belongs to the peculiar kind of cultural animals we are to sit somewhat loose to our cultural determinants. This is not something over and above our cultural determination, just part of the way it functions. It is not something which transcends our culture, but something which is constitutive of it. It is not an ironic attitude I take up to myself, but part of the nature of selfhood. The 'essential' self is not one beyond cultural shaping, but one which is culturally shaped in a specific, self-reflexive way. What is awry here, as Wittgenstein might have said, is a picture which holds us captive – the latent metaphor of culture as a kind of prison-house.

We are held captive here by an image of captivity. There are different cultures, each of which fashions a distinctive form of selfhood, and the problem is how they can communicate with each other. But to belong to a culture just is to be part of a context which is inherently open-ended.

Like the rough ground of language itself, cultures 'work' exactly because they are porous, fuzzy-edged, indeterminate, intrinsically inconsistent, never quite identical with themselves, their boundaries continually modulating into horizons. They are sometimes, to be sure, mutually opaque; but when they *can* be mutually intelligible it is not by virtue of some shared metalanguage into which both can be translated, any more than English can be translated into Serbo-Croat only by dint of some third discourse which encompasses them both. If the 'other' finally lies beyond my comprehension, it is not because of cultural difference but because he is finally unintelligible to himself as well.

The case is put most suggestively by Slavoj Žižek, one of our leading technicians of otherness. What makes communication between different cultures possible, so Žižek argues, is the fact that the limit which prevents our full access to the Other is *ontological*, not merely epistemological. This sounds like making matters worse rather than better; but Žižek's point is that what makes the Other difficult of access is the fact that he or she is never complete in the first place, never wholly determined by a context but always to some extent 'open' and 'floating'. It would be like failing to grasp the meaning of a foreign word because of its inherent ambiguity, not because of our linguistic incompetence. Every culture, then, has an internal blindspot where it fails to grasp or be at one with itself, and to discern this, in Žižek's view, is to understand that culture most fully.

It is at the point where the Other is dislocated in itself, not wholly bound by its context, that we can encounter it most deeply, since this self-opaqueness is also true of ourselves. I understand the Other when I become aware that what troubles me about it, its enigmatic nature, is a problem for it too. As Žižek puts it: 'The dimension of the Universal thus emerges when the two lacks – mine and that of the Other

– overlap . . . What we and the inaccessible Other share is the empty signifier that stands for the X which eludes both positions'.[5] The universal is that breach or fissure in my identity which opens it up from the inside to the Other, preventing me from fully identifying with any particular context. But this is our way of belonging to a context, not a way of lacking one. It belongs to the human situation to be 'out of joint' with any specific situation. And the violent disruption which follows from this connecting of the universal to a particular content is what we know as the human subject. Human beings move at the conjuncture of the concrete and the universal, body and symbolic medium; but this is not a place where anyone can feel blissfully at home.

Nature, on the other hand, is exactly such at-homeness. It is just that it is not for us, but for those other animals whose bodies are such that they have only a limited power to sit loose to their determining contexts. Which is to say, those animals which do not work primarily by culture. Because they move within a symbolic medium, and because they are of a certain material kind, our own bodies have the capacity to extend themselves far beyond their sensuous limits, in what we know as culture, society or technology. It is because our entry into the symbolic order – language and all it brings in its wake – puts some free play between ourselves and our determinants that we are those internally dislocated, non-self-identical creatures known as historical beings. History is what happens to an animal so constituted as to be able, within limits, to determine its own determinations. What is peculiar about a symbol-making creature is that it is of its nature to transcend itself. It is the sign which opens up that operative distance between ourselves and our material surroundings which allows us to transform them into history. Not just the sign, to be sure, but the way that our bodies are fashioned in the first place, capable of complex labour as well as the communication which must necessarily underpin it. Language helps to release us from the prison-house of our senses, at the same time as it damagingly abstracts us from them.

Like Marx's capitalism, then, language opens up at a stroke new possibilities of communication and new modes of exploitation. The move from the tedious happy garden of sensuous existence to the exhilarating, precarious plane of semiotic life was a *felix culpa*, a Fall up rather than down. Because we are both symbolic and somatic animals, potentially universal but pathetically limited, we have a built-in capacity for hubris. Our symbolic existence, abstracting us from the sensory constraints of our bodies, can lead us to overreach and undo ourselves. Only a linguistic animal could fashion nuclear weapons, and only a material animal could be vulnerable to them. We are not so much splendid syntheses of nature and culture, materiality and meaning, as amphibious animals caught on the hop between angel and beast.

Perhaps this lurks somewhere at the root of our attraction to the aesthetic – to that peculiar form of matter which is magically pliant to meaning, that unity of the sensuous and the spiritual which we fail to achieve in our daily, dualistic lives. If psychoanalytical theory is to be credited, the cranking up of our bodily needs to the level of linguistic demand opens up that way of being forever extrinsic to ourselves which we know as the unconscious. But in this perpetual potential for tragedy lies also the source of our finest achievements. Life as a wombat is a good deal less alarming, but also a good deal less enthralling. Pro-wombat liberals may feel this an excessively patronizing claim, but those who maintain that wombats may secretly lead an internal life of agony and ecstasy are surely mistaken. Only creatures capable of certain complex communications can be said to have an internal life. And only those who can practise such intricate communication can also practise secrecy.

Humans are more destructive than tigers because, among other things, our symbolic powers of abstraction allow us to override sensuous inhibitions on intra-specific killing. If I tried to strangle you with my bare hands I would probably succeed only in being sick, which would be unpleasant for you but hardly lethal. But language allows me to destroy you at long range, where physical inhibitions no longer apply. There is probably no hard-and-fast distinction between linguistic and other animals, but there is an immense abyss between ironic and other animals. Creatures whose symbolic life is rich enough to allow them to be ironic are in perpetual danger.

It is important to see that this capacity for culture and history is not just an addition to our nature, but lies at its core. If, as the culturalists maintain, we really were just cultural beings, or as the naturalists hold, just natural ones, then our lives would be a great deal less fraught. It is the fact that we are cusped between nature and culture – a cusping of considerable interest to psychoanalysis – which is the problem. It is not that culture is our nature, but that it is *of* our nature, which makes our life difficult. Culture does not simply supplant nature; instead, it supplements it in a way which is both necessary and supererogatory. We are not born as cultural beings, nor as self-sufficient natural ones, but as creatures whose helpless physical nature is such that culture is a necessity if we are to survive. Culture is the 'supplement' which plugs a gap at the heart of our nature, and our material needs are then reinflected in its terms.

The playwright Edward Bond speaks of the 'biological expectations' with which we are born – the expectation that the baby's 'unpreparedness will be cared for, that it will be given not only food but emotional reassurance, that its vulnerability will be shielded, that it will be born into a world waiting to receive it, and that knows *how* to receive it'.[6] It is perhaps not surprising, in the light of what we shall see later, that these words occur in Bond's preface to his play *Lear*. Such a society, Bond insists, would constitute a true 'culture' – which is why he refuses the term to contemporary capitalist civilization. Once the baby encounters culture, its nature is transformed rather than abolished. It is not that we have an addition to our physical existence known as meaning, as a chimpanzee might wear a purple waistcoat; it is rather that once meaning supervenes upon our bodily existence, that existence can no longer remain identical with itself. A physical gesture is not a way of by-passing language, since it is only within language that it counts as a gesture.

So much is rightly urged by the culturalists. But culture, for both good and ill, does not have it all its own way. Nature is not just clay in culture's hands, and if it were then the political consequences might well be catastrophic. A culture would be ill-advised to try to suppress the kind of needs we have by virtue of what the young Marx calls our 'species being' – needs such as food, sleep, shelter, warmth, physical integrity, companionship, sexual fulfilment, a degree of personal dignity and security, freedom from pain, suffering and oppression, a modest amount of self-determination and the like. If nature is moulded by culture it is also resistant to it, and one might well expect robust political resistance to such a need-denying regime. Natural needs – needs which we have just by virtue of the sort of bodies we are, whatever myriad cultural forms they may assume – are criterial of political well-being, in the sense that societies which thwart them should be politically opposed.

By contrast, the doctrine that the nature of humanity is culture can be politically conservative. If culture really does shape our nature from the ground up, then there seems nothing in that nature to pit itself against an oppressive culture. Michel Foucault has a related problem in explaining how that which is wholly constituted by power can come to resist it. Of course, a lot of resistance to particular cultures is itself cultural, in the sense that it springs wholly from demands which have been culturally bred. Even so, we should not be too eager to relinquish the political critique implicit in our species being – not least in a world where power protects itself by usurping not just our cultural identities but our physical integrity. It is not in the end by infringing cultural rights, but by torture, armed force and death, that such regimes safeguard their privileges. And it is not the most convincing of cases against torture to claim that it violates my rights as a citizen. That which would violate the rights of any culture whatsoever cannot be arraigned simply on cultural grounds.

The most illuminating theoretical treatise on the interplay of nature and culture is *King Lear.* When Lear's daughter remonstrates with him for keeping a retinue of macho ruffians for which he has no need, Lear responds by appealing to the culture-as-supplementarity case:

> O, reason not the need! Our basest beggars
> Are in the poorest things superfluous.
> Allow not nature more than nature needs,
> Man's life is cheap as beast's.
>
> (Act II, sc. iv)

In this, one of his more luminous moments, Lear sees that it belongs to human nature to generate a certain surplus. It would be unnatural for human beings not to be in excess of themselves, enjoying a superfluity beyond strict material need. Human nature is naturally unnatural, overflowing the measure simply by virtue of what it is. It is this which distinguishes humans from 'beasts', whose lives are rigorously determined by their species-needs. There is no *reason* for this tendency in us to exceed the minimal requirements of physical survival; it is just part of the way we are constructed that demand should outstrip need, that culture should be of our nature. A certain lavishness is built in to what we are, so that any actual situation is bound to secrete unrealized potential. It is by virtue of this that we are historical animals.

How much lavishness, though? *King Lear* is among other things a meditation on the difficulty of answering this question without being either niggardly or extravagant. Our most obvious surplus over sheer bodily existence is language, and the play opens with a gross inflation of the stuff. Goneril and Regan, Lear's deceitful daughters, strive to outdo each other in lying rhetoric, betraying by an excess of language a love which is all too little. This verbal spendthriftness then forces their sister Cordelia into a perilous paucity of words, while Lear's own overweening vanity can be chastened only by thrusting him out into a pitiless nature. Nature recalls him to his creaturely existence as a material body, and storm and suffering throw the boundaries of his body into stark exposure. He must learn, in Gloucester's words, to 'see feelingly', shrinking his hubristic consciousness back within the sensuous constraints of the natural body. Only by re-experiencing the body, the medium of our common humanity, will he learn to feel for others in the act of feeling himself.

To be purely bodily, however, is to be no more than a prisoner of one's nature, which is true in the play of Goneril and Regan. There is a thin line between being constrained in the flesh by the needs of others, and being no more than a passive function of one's bodily appetites. If the 'culturalism' of the early Lear puts too much store by signs, titles and power, vainly imagining that representations can determine reality, the naturalism of an operator like Edmund highlights the opposite danger. Edmund is a cynic for whom nature is fact rather than value, meaningless stuff to be manipulated; value for him is just a cultural fiction arbitrarily projected onto the blank text of the world. There is, then, something rather dangerous, as well as admirable, in those who are incapable of being untrue to what they are. Edmund is a full-blooded determinist on this score: 'I should have been that I am, had the maidenliest star in the firmament twinkled on my bastardizing'. And Goneril and Regan, after their initial dissembling, turn out to be as ruthlessly true to their nature as tigers or tornadoes.

Cordelia's inability to falsify herself, by contrast, is a sign of value; but so are redemptive actions of Kent, Edgar and the Fool, who adopt masks, manufacture illusions and play fast and loose with language so as to restore the deranged monarch to his senses. There is a creative as well as a destructive way of sitting loose to one's nature, as the fictions of 'culture' can be harnessed to the cause of bodily compassion. But there is also a creative and destructive way of being true to one's nature. Culture, or human consciousness, must be anchored in the compassionate body to be authentic; the very word 'body' recalls both our individual frailty and our generic being. But culture must not be *reduced* to the natural body, a process of which death is the ultimate symbol, since this can lead either to being a brutish prey to one's own appetites, or to a cynical materialism for which nothing beyond the senses is real. There is a similar problem in the play with language, which as usual in Shakespeare has trouble in finding a mean between being profligate and meagrely functional. Kent's excessively plain speech counterpoints Oswald's foppish idiom, while Goneril's discourse is as relentlessly spare as Edgar's is bemusingly elaborate.

As always with Shakespeare, the concept of surplus is deeply ambivalent. It is at once the mark of our humanity, and what leads us to transgress it. Too much culture shrinks one's capacity for fellow feeling, swaddling one's senses from an exposure to the wretchedness of others. If one could only feel this misery on the body, as Lear learns gropingly to do, then the result would be a surplus in a quite different sense of the word:

> Take physic, pomp;
> Expose thyself to feel what wretches feel,
> That thou mayst shake the superflux to them,
> And show the heavens more just . . .
>
> (Act III, sc. iv)

> Let the superfluous and lust-dieted man
> That slaves your ordinance, that will not see
> Because he does not feel, feel your power quickly;
> So distribution should undo excess,
> And each man have enough.
>
> (Act IV, sc. i)

Lear himself is so far gone in superfluity, so alienated from the real by his crazed desire, that to cure him will mean violently stripping him down to nature, a process he fails to survive. But a rather more constructive way of shedding this surplus is by what the British Labour Party in its better days used to call a fundamental, irreversible redistribution of wealth. The political implications of the drama's meditation on nature and culture are thoroughly egalitarian. There is a creative as well as an injurious superabundance, which is finally symbolized by Cordelia's act of forgiving her father. Mercy for Shakespeare is an overflowing the measure, a refusal of the tit-for-tat of exchange-value, a gratuitousness which is nonetheless necessary.

Rather like the young Marx of the *Economic and Philosophical Manuscripts*, *King Lear* conjures up a radical politics out of its reflections on the body. But this is not quite the discourse of the body which is most in vogue today. It is the mortal body, not the masochistic one, which is in question here. If *Lear* is well aware of nature as a cultural construct, it is also alert to the limits of that ideology, which in its haste to sidestep the pitfalls of naturalism overlooks what it is about the shared, vulnerable, decaying, natural, stubbornly material body which hangs a question mark over such culturalist hubris. But the play is equally wary of a naturalism which believes that there can be a direct inference from fact to value, or from nature to culture. It knows that 'nature' is always an interpretation of nature, all the way from Edmund's Hobbesian determinism to Cordelia's bountiful pastoralism, from a prospect of meaningless matter to a vision of cosmic harmony. The shift from nature to culture cannot be one from fact to value, since nature is always already a value-term.

This, then, is the rock upon which any naturalistic ethics would seem to founder. We cannot, it would appear, argue our way up from how it is with us as material bodies to what we ought to do, since our account of how it is with us will always be inescapably evaluative. It is this which licenses the culturalist epistemology for which there is no such thing as what is the case, just what is the case for some partisan observer. Like culture, the concept of nature hovers ambiguously between the descriptive and the normative. If human nature is a purely descriptive category, covering whatever it is that human beings do, then we cannot derive values from it, since what we do is varied and contradictory. If, as popular wisdom has it, it is 'human' to be morally frail, it is equally 'human' to be compassionate. But if human nature is already a value-term, then the process of deriving moral and political values from it would seem pointlessly circular.

Shakespeare seems aware of this dilemma in his own way, but is reluctant to take the culturalist road out of it. That simply lands one up in as many philosophical difficulties as naturalism. It is just as implausible to see culture as a mere outcropping of nature as it is to view Nature as a mere construct of culture. Shakespeare clings quite properly to a notion of human nature which is communal, somatically based and culturally mediated. He also believes that the finest cultural values are somehow rooted in this nature. Compassion, for example, is a moral value, but one which takes its cue from the fact that we are by our very constitution social animals who are materially capable of sympathizing with one another's needs, and must do so in order to survive. It is this sort of internal relation between fact and value, culture and nature, which lies at the heart of *Lear*'s reflections. Yet the fact that we are by nature mutually sympathetic animals does not of course mean that we always practise compassion in the moral sense of the term. Far from it. All the anti-culturalist claims is that when we *do* feel for others in this normative sense, we are realizing a capacity which belongs to our nature, rather than simply exercising a virtue which descends to us from a purely contingent cultural tradition.

This, however, leaves open the question of how we identify those capacities of our nature which are morally and politically most positive. And here the culturalist is right to claim that this cannot be done by some process of logical inference, or by delivering a value-free account of nature which would nevertheless impel us in one cultural direction rather than another. In the end, we can establish this only by argument and evidence. And it is here, unexpectedly, that culture in the more specialist sense of the word plays its part. If one thinks of the range of artistic works, both 'high' and popular, which have generally been thought valuable, it is remarkable what common witness they bear on the question of what moral ends are to be promoted.

This testimony is by no means unanimous or unequivocal: there are some powerful pieces of artistic culture which advocate moral values which are at best dubious and at worst obnoxious. And high culture itself, as we have seen, is deeply embroiled in exploitation and unhappiness. Even so, there are strikingly few cherished works of art which advocate torture and mutilation as the surest way of flourishing, or celebrate rapine and famine as the most precious of human experiences. This fact is so baldly obvious that we are tempted to pass over its curiousness. For why, from a culturalist or historicist standpoint, should this be so? Why this imposing consensus? If we really are nothing but our local, ephemeral cultural conditions, of which there have been countless millions in the history of the species, how come that artistic culture over the ages does not affirm almost as many different moral values? Why is it that, with some egregious exceptions and in countless different cultural modes, culture in this sense has not on the whole elevated rapacious egoism over loving kindness, or material acquisitiveness over generosity?

That culture is an arena of exceptionally complex moral wrangling is not to be doubted: what the ancient sagas affirm as virtuous is not necessarily what Thomas Pynchon does. What counts as cruelty or kindness is what cultures argue over, and here there can be sizeable discrepancies between, say, ancient slave-owners and modern liberals. There can just as easily be conflicts within a single culture. Lear thinks it unkind of Cordelia to declare that she loves him 'according to her bond', but this is kindness in the strictest possible sense: she means that her feelings for him spring from the demands of kinship, which entails that she will treat him humanely however he may treat her. Yet at the broadest level there are some remarkable consistencies of moral judgement between cultures, which cannot simply be set aside in glib historicist fashion. And this comes as no surprise to the kind of ethical materialist for whom moral values have a relation to our creaturely nature, which has not significantly altered over the ages.

When we engage in argument over what constitutes the good life, our appeal has in the end to be to evidence rather than abstract principles. It is a question of knowing what kind of evidence is cogent enough to convince an opponent. And it is here that culture in the narrower sense is indispensable to the moral or political philosopher. In the end, one cannot produce a knockdown argument; one can only point one's interlocutor towards, say, the corpus of Arabic poetry or the European novel, and ask her what she makes of this. If someone really maintained that evil was an outdated concept, one might save oneself a lot of tedious wrangling by asking whether he had read, say, Primo Levi. Many of today's modish epistemological sceptics, in their theoreticist eagerness to puncture foundationalist claims, seem to forget that this, after all, is how dissent and agreement, conviction and conversion, actually take place, in the real social world if not within the walls of academia.

The liberal humanist, however, should not draw too much consolation from this case. For the liberal humanist's mistake is not to insist that human beings from very different contexts may share values in common, but to imagine that these values are invariably what is most important about a cultural artefact. It is also to assume that they are always, in however cunningly disguised form, the values of his own civilization. The point about the abstract generality of such categories as compassion or generosity is not only that they cry out for cultural specification, which is indeed the case; it is also that they cannot therefore be the possession of any particular culture. This is not, to be sure, what makes them positive, since just the same could be said of violence and hatred; but the culturalist should hesitate before claiming that such values are so general as to be meaningless. So, in that case, are the celebration of difference and the resistance to oppression.

Just as our perceptions inform us that there is more to the world than our perceptions, so an attentive reading of culture suggests that there is more to the world than culture. This, at least, is the conclusion reached by some of the greatest theorists of modernity, whatever some of their postmodern successors may assert. The wager of Marx, Nietzsche and Freud is that at the root of meaning lies a certain *force*, but that only a symptomatic reading of culture will disclose its traces. It is because meanings are always caught up in force – split, garbled and displaced by it – that any mere hermeneutics or theory of interpretation is bound to remain idealist. For these thinkers, all the most significant events move at the uneasy conjuncture of meaning and power, of the semiotic and (in the broadest sense) economic. Men and women do not live by culture alone, not even in the more capacious sense of the term. There is always that within culture which baffles and balks it, twists it into violent or nonsensical speech, or deposits within it a residue of sheer meaninglessness. Whatever is prior to culture, whether it is Kant's transcendental conditions of possibility, Nietzsche's will to power, Marx's material history, Freud's primary processes or Lacan's Real, is always in a sense simultaneous with it too, since we can identify it only by reading it off from culture itself. Whatever puts culture in place and perpetually threatens to undo it can only, so to speak, be reconstructed backwards once culture has already happened. In this sense, to be sure, it does not escape meaning; but neither is it reducible to the symbolic realm.

For Marx, culture has only one origin, and that is labour upon nature. That labour for Marxism means exploitation is one meaning of Walter Benjamin's wise dictum that every document of civilization is also a record of barbarism. Culture for Marx is generally ignorant of its parentage: like the Oedipalized child, it prefers to believe that it sprang from an altogether superior sort of lineage, if not fully armed from its own head. What gives birth to culture, however, is not meaning but need. It is only later, when society has evolved to the point where it can support a full-time institutional culture, that culture comes to assume a real autonomy of practical life. For Marxism, this autonomy is an historical fact rather than a formalist illusion.

Just as labour involves an encounter of power and meaning, so does ideology. Ideology happens wherever power impacts upon signification, bending it out of shape or hooking it up to a cluster of interests. Walter Benjamin remarked that myth would endure as long as the last beggar, meaning no doubt that ideology is indispensable as long as there is injustice. Marxism looks to a time when men and women will be able to live largely by culture, free of the goad of material necessity. But if its governing trope is irony, it is because it understands that to sit loose to material necessity requires certain material preconditions. For social life to be aestheticized – for men and women to deploy their powers largely for their own self-delight, rather than simply to stay alive – cannot be achieved by aesthetics alone.

History for Marx, that nightmare weighing upon the brains of the living, is more properly 'pre-history', while Nietzsche speaks scoffingly of 'that gruesome dominion of nonsense and accident that has so far been called "history" '.[7] Nietzsche's own preferred term – genealogy – stands for that barbarous narrative of debt, torture and revenge of which culture is the blood-stained fruit. 'Every small step on earth has been paid for by spiritual and physical torture . . . how much blood and cruelty lies at the bottom of all "good things"!'.[8] Genealogy unmasks the disreputable origins of noble ideas, the chanciness of their functions, lighting up the murky underside of thought. Morality for Nietzsche is really sublimation, as indeed it is for Freud. Yet this makes it more, not less, authentic. As William Empson wisely remarks, 'the most refined desires are inherent in the plainest, and would be false if they weren't'.[9] The mode of thought which understands this most is the carnivalesque.

Freud's originality is to see not just culture or morality in these terms, but civilization as a whole. If the Sistine chapel is sublimation, so is the manufacture of scooters. Freud's boldest move here is to dismantle the whole classical opposition between 'culture' and 'civil society', the realm of value and the kingdom of necessity. Both have their unlovely roots in *Eros*. Meanings for Freud are certainly meanings, to be patiently deciphered; but to flip this whole process over is also to see it as a mighty warring of somatic forces. Culture and nature, the semiotic and the somatic, meet only in conflict: the body is never quite at home in the symbolic order, and will never entirely recover from its traumatic insertion into it. The Freudian drive lies somewhere on the shadowy border between body and mind, representing the one to the other at the troubled crossroads between nature and culture. Freud is a 'culturalist' in so far as the body for him is always a fictional representation; but the bad news which this representation has to deliver is of forces which warp our cultural meanings from within, and which threaten in the end to sink them without trace.

So much is clear from *Civilisation and Its Discontents*, that remorselessly bleak treatise for which all civilization is ultimately self-marring. Freud posits in us both a primary aggression and a primary narcissism, and civilization is conjured out of a sublimation of both. It involves a renunciation of instinctual gratification, so that culture, far from harmoniously developing our powers, leads us to what Freud calls a state of 'permanent internal unhappiness'. On this view, the fruits of culture are not so much truth, goodness and beauty as guilt, sadism and self-destructiveness. It is *Eros*, builder of cities, which dominates nature and creates a culture; but it does this by fusing with our aggressivity, within which lurks *Thanatos* or the death drive. What destroys civilization is thus duped out of its nefarious intentions and harnessed to the business of establishing it. But the more we sublimate *Eros* in this way, the more we deplete its resources and leave it a prey to the sadistic superego. By strengthening the superego, we deepen our guilt and foster a lethal culture of self-loathing. Culture is driven in part by that which lies beyond all culture, death. If death drives us forward, it is only to return us to that blissful state of invulnerability before culture ever emerged.

These, then, are among the lessons of late modernity. There are forces at work within culture – desire, dominion, violence, vindictiveness – which threaten to unravel our meanings, capsize our projects, draw us inexorably back into darkness. These forces do not exactly fall outside culture; they spring up, rather, at its troubled interface with nature. For Marx, labour is a form of intercourse with nature which produces a culture; but because of the conditions under which this labour takes place, that culture is internally split into violence and contradiction. For Nietzsche, our fight for dominion over nature involves a potentially catastrophic sovereignty over ourselves, as we degut ourselves of instinct in the struggle for civility. For Freud, the traffic between the infant's body and those surrounding it, the necessary business of caring and nurture without which we shall die, sows the seeds of a ravenous desire for which no body and no object will ever provide adequate fulfilment.

Nature is not just the Other of culture. It is also a kind of inert weight within it, opening up an inner fracture which runs all the way through the human subject. We can wrest culture out of Nature only by harnessing some of our own natural energies to the task; cultures are not in this sense built by purely cultural means. But these dominative energies then tend to set up a well-nigh unstoppable momentum which is far in excess of what culture needs to survive, and which we can also turn with equal aggressiveness upon ourselves. In this light, there is always something ultimately self-undoing about the making of cultures.

The Italian philosopher Sebastiano Timpanaro writes that

> love, the brevity and frailty of human existence, the contrast between the smallness and weakness of man and the infinity of the cosmos, are expressed in literary works in very different ways in various historically determinate societies, but still not in such different ways that all reference to such constant experiences of the human condition as the sexual instinct, the debility produced by age (with its psychological repercussions), the fear of one's own death and sorrow at the death of others, is lost.[10]

In the dogmatic culturalism of our day, such judiciousness is rare. Instead, the suffering, mortal, needy, desiring body which links us fundamentally with our historical ancestors, as well as with our fellow beings from other cultures, has been converted into a principle of cultural difference and division. The body has a curiously dual status, as at once universal and individual. Indeed the word 'body' itself can denote either the singular or the collective. It is the inherited, sheerly given stuff which links us to our species, as implacably impersonal as the unconscious, a destiny which we were never allowed to choose. To this extent, it is the symbol of our solidarity. But the body is also individual – indeed is arguably the very principle of individuation. It is because the body is discrete, local and drastically limited, not literally locked into the body of its species, that we are so fearfully vulnerable. It is also because as infants we are almost, but never quite, locked into the bodies of others that we end up so needy and desirous.

To compensate for that fragility, human bodies need to construct those forms of solidarity we call culture, which are considerably more elaborate than anything that the body can do directly, but perilously beyond its sensuous control. A common culture can be fashioned only because our bodies are of broadly the same kind, so that the one universal rests upon the other. Sociality bears in upon us as individuals at a level even deeper than culture, as the young Marx recognized. Of course human bodies differ, in their history, gender, ethnicity, physical capacities and the like. But they do not differ in those capacities – language, labour, sexuality – which enable them to enter into potentially universal relationship with one another in the first place. The postmodern cult of the socially constructed body, for all its resourceful critique of naturalism, has been closely linked with the abandonment of the very idea of a politics of global resistance – and this in an age when the politics of global domination are more importunate than ever.

5

Towards a Common Culture

We have seen that culture as civility and culture as solidarity are for the most part sworn enemies. But they can also strike up some strange, potent alliances, as they do in the work of T.S. Eliot.[1] Eliot may be a connoisseur of high culture, but he is also a champion of culture as popular way of life; like all the most intelligent elitists, he is also a full-blooded populist. There is no logical contradiction between these cases, whatever postmodern theory might consider.

Eliot's writings on culture superbly illustrate the constant sliding of the concept. What he means by culture, he announces, is 'first of all what the anthropologists mean: the way of life of a particular people living together in one place'.[2] But at other times culture as a value-term seems uppermost in his mind – 'Culture may even be described simply as that which makes life worth living' (p. 27) – while floating between these two meanings is a sense of culture as the whole complex of a society's arts, manners, religion and ideas, which can be pressed into the service of either definition. The culture of a society is at one point 'that which makes it a society' (p. 37), though we are told elsewhere, contradictorily, that it is possible to anticipate a period 'of which it is possible to say that it will have *no* culture' (p. 19). Eliot sometimes exploits the word's ambiguity quite deliberately, as when he speaks of 'the hereditary transmission of culture within a culture' (p. 32).

Raymond Williams has pointed out that when Eliot comes to spell out what he means by culture as a way of life, he lists a selection of topics – Derby Day, Henley Regatta, Cowes, boiled cabbage, Elgar – which amount ironically to the *alternative* definition of culture: in Williams's wry phrase, 'sport, food, a little art'.[3] The shift, in fact, has an interestingly mystificatory effect. Eliot wants to argue that minority culture benefits culture as a whole; but the plausibility of this case depends upon what one means by minority culture. If culture means the arts and intellectual life, then it is feasible to claim that, in fostering these, the cultural elite might finally enhance society as a whole. But if upper-class culture includes, say, the Enclosure Acts and private medical insurance, it is harder to see quite how these constitute an enrichment of all social levels.

Culture for Eliot is not only a way of life, but 'the *whole way of life* of a people, from birth to the grave, from morning to night and even in sleep' (p. 31). Especially in sleep, one might add. For the point about this sense of culture for Eliot is that it is far more unconscious than conscious. A culture, he comments, 'can never be wholly conscious – there is always more to it than we are conscious of; and it cannot be planned because it is always the unconscious background of all our planning . . . Culture cannot altogether be brought to consciousness; and the culture of which we are wholly conscious is never the whole of culture' (pp. 94, 107). This is a just perception, but also a convenient one. A culture for Eliot, rather like a form of life for Wittgenstein, cannot itself be wholly objectified because it is the transcendental condition of all our objectifications. In Heideggerian terms, it is the set of 'pre-understandings' which allow specific acts of understanding to happen in the first place, and so cannot itself be entirely grasped by them. But if this is also a convenient position for Eliot to take, it is because his commitment to the idea of popular culture is at odds with his conservative estimate of popular capacities. For Eliot, humankind cannot bear very much reality, and neither can they rise to much intelligent thought. It follows that popular culture, to exist at all, has to be a largely unconscious affair – and 'culture' is on hand as a word which suggests, as well as a fineness of living, a process lived on the pulses rather than in the mind. As Eliot writes, in odiously patronizing style:

> For the great mass of humanity whose attention is occupied mostly by their direct relation to the soil, or the sea, or the machine, and to a small number of persons, pleasures and duties, two conditions (for a Christian culture) are required. The first is that, as their capacity for *thinking* about the objects of faith is small, their Christianity may be almost wholly realised in behaviour: both in their customary and periodic religious observances, and in a traditional code of behaviour towards their neighbours. The second is that, while they should have some perception of how far their lives fall short of Christian ideals, their religious and social life should form for them a natural whole, so that the difficulty of behaving as Christians should not impose an intolerable strain.[4]

It is the tone of an author who announces elsewhere that 'on the whole, it would appear to be for the best that the great majority of human beings should go on living in the place in which they were born' (p. 52). It was not a piece of advice he observed himself. What Eliot means in the passage quoted above is that you can be a dedicated Christian while hardly realizing it at all. Culture must be largely a matter of ritual observance and behaviour, since most people lack the capacity for any very remarkable self-consciousness. One is reminded of Louis Althusser's definition of ideology as spontaneous conduct, which takes a similarly religious form:

> The individual in question behaves in such and such a way, adopts such and such a practical attitude, and, what is more, participates in certain regular practices which are those of the ideological apparatus on which 'depend' the ideas which he has in all consciousness freely chosen as a subject. If he believes in God, he goes to Church to attend Mass, kneels, prays, confesses, does penance (once it was material in the ordinary sense of the term) and naturally repents, and so on.[5]

In Althusser's view, ideology is more a matter of practices than ideas: there is an implicit distinction here between the ideology of the masses and the theory of the intelligentsia. Eliot, similarly, by no means disowns the idea of culture as consciousness; it is just that this is the monopoly of an educated coterie. Althusser's theoreticians become Eliot's secular priesthood. But the people and the intelligentsia do not constitute *different* cultures. The same culture will be lived out unconsciously by the people and self-reflectively by the minority. A common culture is thus entirely compatible with a hierarchical one. The difference that matters is not between kinds of culture, but between degrees of self-consciousness. The great majority of people believe without knowing that they do. A unity of belief and behaviour is the condition of a healthy popular culture, but hardly of a spiritually aware individual. It is the tension between the two which characterizes the finely conscious elect, struggling as they do with their sense of falling short of ideals which finally transcend any common life. Dislocation of conduct and consciousness is thus a mark of spiritual superiority; the two are unified only in the savage or the saint.

Eliot confesses in *Notes Towards the Definition of Culture* that

> The reflection that . . . even the most conscious and developed of us live also at the level on which belief and behaviour cannot be distinguished, is one that may, once we allow our imagination to play on it, be very disconcerting . . . To reflect that from one point of view religion is culture, and from another point of view culture is religion, can be very disturbing. (p. 32)

Culture is *habitus*, in Pierre Bourdieu's term,[6] but it is also, contradictorily, the most finely self-reflective existence of which we are capable. As we saw in chapter 1, the very word includes both organic growth and the active tending of it. And Eliot seems perturbed by this blending of the speculative and the spontaneous. How can culture be at once what we don't need to think about, and the finest fruits of our consciousness? If religion, or high culture, is rooted in culture as way of life, then it risks being reducible to it, and its transcendent value is accordingly lost. Yet if it does not have such everyday roots, how can it be effective? Similarly, if my beliefs are just another way of describing my behavioural habits, then they would seem reassuringly well grounded, but only at the price of ceasing to be commitments on which I can be congratulated, any more than I can be congratulated on my tendency to snore. Eliot remarks that 'behaviour is as potent to affect belief, as belief to affect behaviour':[7] culture as conduct is what entrenches in the lives of the many a set of beliefs fostered by the few. But the problem is to embody belief in behaviour while avoiding the disturbing corollary that behaviour may exhaust belief. Besides, the beliefs in question, whether religious or aesthetic, finally transcend everyday life altogether, so their incarnation in it can only ever be partial. What allows these beliefs to criticize everyday life is thus also what fails to anchor them securely in it.

Eliot, then, has his own version of the Culture/culture problem, but his own solution too. He cannot opt in purely elitist manner for Culture as against culture, since he is shrewd enough to recognize that no minority culture will survive unless it sends down complex shoots into popular life. Only in this way will high culture become a *political* force in an age of distasteful mass democracy. But how can high culture do this if the great majority of men and women can hardly think at all? Eliot is dismayed by the prospect of a society in which 'our headlong rush to educate everybody' is simply preparing the ground 'upon which the barbarian nomads of the future will encamp in their mechanised caravans' (p. 108); but he is right to see that the embattled Leavisian response to this catastrophe – batten down the high-cultural hatches and train a minority in cultural self-defence – is hardly a sufficient strategy.

Eliot is not prepared to throw in the cultural towel so quickly; but he sees that if Culture is once more to exert its influence on the masses, it will have to be in the form of religious culture. His religious conservatism is thus both more and less realistic than Leavis's secular liberalism: more so, since it recognizes that the common people are swayed not by works of literature but by ways of life; less so, in that the particular way of life Eliot espouses – Christianity – had been rapidly losing ground with the masses for at least a century. Even so, it is religion above all which unites reflective awareness with spontaneous conduct, and this unity can be directly mapped on to a hierarchical social order. A priestlike clerisy, composed of individuals not utterly dissimilar to T.S. Eliot, will consciously nourish spiritual values, but these will be disseminated to the people and lived out by them obliquely, unreflectively, in the rhythm and texture of their lived experience. Culture for most people is a ritual of unconscious conformism. There can be no question of any direct offering of the values of the minority to the masses: 'to aim to make everyone share in the appreciation of the fruits of the more conscious part of culture is to adulterate and cheapen what you give' (pp. 106–7).

For Eliot, then, a common culture is by no means an egalitarian one. If the minority and the masses share common values, they do so at different levels of consciousness. 'According to my view of culture', Eliot writes in *Notes Towards the Definition of Culture*, 'the whole of the population *should* take an active part in cultural activities – not all in the same activities or on the same level' (p. 38). Readers of Eliot's own poetry can be ranked in a similar way, a few of them grasping the erudite allusions to fertility cults or the *Aeneid* while the majority are simply moved in their visceral regions by the haunting enigmas of the imagery. As a full-blooded populist who celebrated jazz and music hall, Eliot believes the latter sort of audience far more important, since culture, or ideology, operates through the gut rather than the mind. He is genuinely nonchalant about the paraphrasable meaning of his own poetry, which is one reason why the notes to *The Waste Land* are spoof.

In Eliot's ideal society, then, all social classes will share the same culture, but the task of the elite will be 'to bring about a further development of the culture in organic complexity: culture at a more conscious level, but still the same culture' (p. 37). As a convinced anti-bourgeois, Eliot rejects the liberal theory of society, of equality of opportunity and meritocratic elites, as an atomistic doctrine which destroys both common belief and the continuity essential for genuine cultural transmission. Instead, the traditional governing class, by preserving and transmitting its culture from generation to generation, will be the tip of developed spiritual and artistic consciousness, and as such will be sustaining not merely itself, but the culture as a whole.

The upper cultural levels will not possess more culture than the lower, simply 'a more conscious culture and a greater specialisation of culture' (p. 48). The two central meanings of the word 'culture' are thus socially distributed: culture as a body of artistic and intellectual work is the preserve of the elite, while culture in its anthropological sense belongs to the common people. What is vital, however, is that these two forms of culture interbreed: 'this higher level of culture', Eliot notes, 'must be thought of both as valuable in itself, and as an enriching of the lower levels: thus the movement of culture would proceed in a kind of cycle, each class nourishing the others' (p. 37).

In a venerable tradition from Edmund Burke, 'culture' here signifies those habits of feeling which bind us, largely unconsciously, to a traditional form of life. As the anti-rationalist Eliot recognizes, these are far more compelling than culture as mere ideas. Ideas are the currency of the rationalist left, whereas culture epitomizes all that conservatism offers in their place: custom, manners, tradition, instinct, reverence. An industry, Eliot suggests, 'if it is to engage the interest of more than the conscious mind of the worker, should also have a way of life somewhat peculiar to its initiates, with its own forms of festivity and observances' (p. 16n). One imagines cross-gartered coal miners with bells on their knees. But the political left, embarrassingly enough, has also traditionally adhered to a common culture, and seen ideas as subservient to material life. If Eliot values the unconscious components of culture, so does Raymond Williams:

> A culture, while it is being lived, is always in part unknown, in part unrealised. The making of a community is always an exploration, for consciousness cannot precede creation, and there is no formula for unknown experience. A good community, a living culture, will, because of this, not only make room for but actively encourage all and any who can contribute to the advance in consciousness which is the common need . . . We need to consider every attachment, every value, with our whole attention; for we do not know the future, we may never be certain of what may enrich it.[8]

For Williams, a culture can never be brought fully to consciousness because it is never fully achieved. What is constitutively open-ended can never be completely totalized. Culture is a network of shared meanings and activities never self-conscious as a whole, but growing towards the 'advance in consciousness', and thus in full humanity, of a whole society. A common culture involves the collaborative making of such meanings, with the full participation of all its members; and this is the key difference between Williams's and Eliot's idea of a common culture. For Williams, a culture is common only when it is collectively made; for Eliot, a culture is common even when its making is reserved to the privileged few. For Williams, a common culture is one which is continuously remade and redefined by the collective practice of its members, not one in which values framed by the few are then taken over and passively lived by the many. For this, he prefers the term 'culture in common'.

Williams's notion of a common culture is thus inseparable from radical socialist change. It requires an ethic of common responsibility, full democratic participation at all levels of social life, including material production, and egalitarian access to the culture-fashioning process. But the product of this conscious political activity is, ironically, a certain unconsciousness. Williams's common culture is both more and less conscious than Eliot's: more so, because it involves the active participation of all its members; less so, because what will be produced by this collaboration can be neither drafted in advance nor fully known in the making. This involves a logical inference rather than a moral exhortation: a culture fashioned by an elite can be known and predicted in a way that one shaped by an immensely complex collaboration cannot. Williams makes the point by mobilizing the 'unconscious' component of the term 'culture':

> We have to plan what can be planned, according to our common decision. But the emphasis of the idea of culture is right when it reminds us that a culture, essentially, is unplannable. We have to ensure the means of life, and the means of community. But what will then, by these means, be lived, we cannot know

> or say. The idea of culture rests on a metaphor: the tending of natural growth. And indeed it is on growth, as metaphor and as fact, that the ultimate emphasis must be placed.[9]

Rather than piously dismissing the organic metaphor as insidiously naturalizing, Williams retrieves from it its radical potential. Culture as an idea is deployed against the left rationalists; but since what makes it unplannable is the diverse participation it demands, it is brandished equally against the Burkeian conservatives. A common culture could never be wholly self-transparent precisely because of the range of active collaboration it engages, not because it betrays the enigmatic mystery of an organism. Consciousness and unconsciousness are for Williams thus aspects of the same process, whereas for Eliot they are qualities of different social groups. Eliot may be much possessed by ideas of organic culture, but since his conception of culture is elitist he can, ironically, prescribe its content much more determinately than Williams can. The values in question are those of an existing coterie, and will not suffer significant modification in being transmitted to the people. It is, rather, their form which will alter. Both Eliot and Williams point to the values of an existing social class as proleptic of the future: with Eliot, the aristocracy and right-wing intelligentsia; with Williams, the working-class movement, whose ethic of solidarity and cooperative institutions prefigure a more inclusive common culture. But whereas Williams envisages these values, once extended to other groups, as undergoing a radical reworking, rejecting as he does any simple-minded panacea of 'proletarian culture', Eliot anticipates no such transformation. Indeed the majority of people are in his view too dim-witted to achieve it. Since the people are excluded from the active (re-)making of meanings and values, the essentials of a common culture can already be prescribed. Eliot does not need to wait upon what will emerge from a common collaboration, since in his scheme there will be no such collaboration.

Williams sees that given values, once proffered to new social groups, end up as non-self-identical, since reception is always refashioning. It is a point less luminously grasped by those cultural populists for whom making Pushkin available to the people is not only patronizing but superfluous, since Pushkin is of no relevance to them. Like elitists, such populists assume that cultural meanings are fixed. Like elitists too, they confuse 'bourgeois culture', in the sense of doctrines like possessive individualism which are inherently of that origin, with values like the appreciation of Verdi, which by and large have been confined to that class but have no inherent need to be. For Eliot, by contrast, there can be no question of high-cultural values, once distilled in the unconscious conduct of the masses, undergoing significant alteration. Both Eliot and Williams contrast a *common* culture with a *uniform* one: both stress the unevenness and plurality of any actual culture. But for Eliot, that unevenness springs ironically from a rigid structure of levels: all will not experience alike because all will not participate alike. Williams, while agreeing that full participation in the whole culture by any one individual is out of the question, sees the diversity of a common culture as the result of its involving so many agents. What we can expect is 'not a simple equality (in the sense of identity) of culture; but rather a very complex system of specialised developments – the whole of which will form the whole culture, but which will not be available or conscious, as a whole, to any individual or group living within it'.[10] Whereas for Eliot the culture is common in content, being royalist, ruralist and Anglo-Catholic, its commonness for Williams lies chiefly in its political form. And this common participatory form is not only compatible with a plurality of cultural experience, but logically entails it.

Williams's conception of a common culture thus sheds new light on the current debates between pluralists and communitarians,[11] culture as hybridity and culture as identity. Eliot, one might claim, is a kind of proto-communitarian, advocating a community of belief and a shared cultural pedigree. Today's opponents of this case include both classical liberals and postmodern pluralists, cases which share more in common than perhaps either camp would wish to acknowledge. Williams's theory of a common culture, however, cannot be aligned on this axis. It cannot be dismissed by the postmodernists as organicist nostalgia, partly because it involves political transformations whose full implications are revolutionary, partly because it sees culture not as an integrated whole but as 'a very complex system of specialised developments'. If it is a common culture, it is not a corporate one. But neither can the case be unreservedly embraced by the radical hybridists and liberal pluralists, since it involves a communality of belief and action which is hardly to their taste. The paradox of Williams's position is that the conditions for this complex cultural development can be laid only by politically securing what he rather evasively calls the 'means of community', by which he means, in effect, socialist institutions. And this certainly involves common belief, commitment and practice. Only through a fully participatory democracy, including one which regulated material production, could the channels of access be fully opened to give vent to this cultural diversity. To establish genuine cultural pluralism, in brief, requires concerted socialist action. It is precisely this that contemporary culturalism fails to see. Williams's position would no doubt seem to it quaintly residual, not to say positively archaic; the problem in fact is that we have yet to catch up with it.

For Williams, then, what matters most is not cultural politics, but the politics of culture. Politics are the condition of which culture is the product. Since he rejects any vulgar-Marxist notion of culture as 'secondary', he regards this not as an ontological doctrine but as a practical imperative. Eliot, who as a Tory is committed in practice to an individualist social order which runs contrary to his cultural ideal, fatally overlooks this order of priorities. So indeed does a good deal of today's identity politics. The very notion of liberating cultural difference implies that this is a good all round, which in turn implies a politics of universal equality. To this, ironically, many devotees of identity politics are either hostile or indifferent. But there is no 'cultural politics', in the sense of certain forms of politics which are specifically cultural. On the contrary, culture is not inherently political at all. There is nothing inherently political in singing a Breton love-song, staging an exhibition of African-American art or declaring oneself a lesbian. These things are not innately and eternally political; they become so only under specific historical conditions, usually of an unpleasant kind. They become political only when they are caught up in a process of domination and resistance – when these otherwise innocuous matters are turned for one reason or another into terrains of struggle. The ultimate point of a politics of culture is to restore to them their innocuousness, so that one can sing, paint or make love without the bothersome distraction of political strife. It is true that there are proponents of identity politics who will then have no idea what to do with themselves, but this is their problem, not ours.

Williams's well-known distinction between residual, dominant and emergent forms of culture finds some echo in the concerns of this book. The residual, he insists, is not the same as the archaic, though in practice the two are often difficult to distinguish. Unlike the archaic, the residual is still an active element of the present, an expression of values and experiences which a dominant culture fails fully to accommodate. Among his examples of such formations, Williams offers rural community and organized religion. A good deal of culture as identity or solidarity is in this sense residual – enclaves of traditionalist resistance within the present which draw their strength from 'some previous social and cultural institution or formation',[12] and which in Williams's terms can be either 'oppositional' or 'alternative'. If nationalism is among other things an oppositional form of residual culture, New Ageism is an alternative one. But such movements are also products of the present, as well as potential harbingers of the future. Indeed what has come about in our time could be seen as an increasingly close interweaving of all three of Williams's categories. The dominant culture, itself an unequal composite of the 'high' and the postmodern, of civility and commercialism, increasingly undermines traditional identities, thus pressurizing the residual to the point where it reappears as the emergent. The beleaguered family, region, community, moral code, religious tradition, ethnic group, nation-state or natural environment inspires a movement which in challenging the dominant culture of the present, lays claim to what might lie beyond it. While postmodernism declares an end to history, these forces continue to act out that more modernist scenario in which the past returns, this time as the future.

What placed the topic of culture most immediately on the agenda for our age was no doubt the culture industry – the fact that, in an historic post-war development, culture has now become thoroughly locked into the general process of commodity production. But this is simply part of a lengthier, more complex narrative of our times, bringing to consummation a burgeoning of 'mass' culture which can be traced back at least to the *fin de siècle*. In the early decades of the twentieth century, arguments about culture were really about this momentous evolution, which seemed to many to presage the death of civility itself. The debates, in short, were largely centred on 'high' versus 'mass' culture, and the elegaic tones of this *Kulturpessimismus*, which reverberate today in the melancholic work of George Steiner, were re-echoed from Oswald Spengler to Ortega y Gasset, F.R. Leavis to Max Horkheimer, Lionel Trilling to Richard Hoggart. What most of these debates passed over was the fact that an art which was both taxingly complex and politically subversive had indeed thrived briefly, and its name was the avant garde. It was partly because this avant garde had collapsed under political pressure that 'high' art now seemed so painfully disconnected from popular currents.

The name of Hoggart, however, marks a significant shift of perspective. For *The Uses of Literacy* was, so to speak, a *Kulturpessimismus* of the left, at once a late document in this old lineage and an early essay in a new one. The threatened culture to be mourned was no longer high European humanism but the proletarian life of the north of England. Hoggart's magnificently original work appeared roughly at the same time as Williams's *Culture and Society 1780–1950*, but in the latter book the decisive transition had been made. The idea of culture was now reappropriated by the political left, both as a response to a new kind of post-war capitalism in which the media and consumerism bulked increasingly large, and as a way of distancing oneself from Stalinism. There was, in fact, a rich heritage of leftist cultural writing, both inside and outside the Communist parties, which had certainly not leapt into being with the New Left; but a generation of ex-working-class, largely non-Communist Western intellectuals in search of a fresh political alignment could find it among other places in the concept of culture, which conveniently linked their humanistic training to the new social currents of the post-war West. The peace movement provided another such point of identity, at a stage of the Cold War when the survival of culture in any sense of the word seemed in doubt.

This theoretical *rapprochement* between politics and culture was soon to find its fleshly incarnation in the cultural politics of the 1960s. But as those political hopes receded, the culture industry expanded throughout the 1970s and 1980s until a new term was needed for the phenomenon it signified: postmodernism. What the word signalled, in effect, was that the old-style *Kulturkampf* between minority civilization and mass barbarism was now officially over. The 1960s had challenged patrician art in the name of the populist and subversive, but what had now triumphed could no longer quite be captured by either category. If it was populist, it was scarcely subversive. It included high art, but one now fully locked into commodity production; it spanned highly sophisticated 'mass' culture and *schlock* and *kitsch*, avant-garde experiment and commercial banality.

There were still distinctions of high and low; but traditional high culture, still with some strong class resonances, was now increasingly sidelined, while there was now almost no popular culture outside commercial forms. Instead, the high/low distinctions were themselves largely relocated within a hybrid, cross-cutting culture which spread its influence indifferently into every social enclave, rather than as a hierarchy of isolated, mutually uncomprehending universes. This was not, in fact, a wholly novel development. The traditional class structure, and the traditional cultural pecking order, had never been simply correlated; the aristocracy has not been remarkable for its love of Schoenberg. High culture was always the stomping ground of the intelligentsia rather than a narrowly class affair, though the intelligentsia itself is usually that. Postmodern culture, conversely, is classless in the sense that consumerism is classless, which is to say that it cuts across class divisions while driving a system of production which finds such divisions indispensable. In any case, the consumption of a classless culture is nowadays increasingly the mark of the middle class.

Something more, however, was needed to qualify for the 'post-modern' brand-name. What was felt to have altered was not just the content of culture, but its status. It was its transformative influence on other levels of society which mattered, not just the fact that it was looming larger. What was taking place, in Fredric Jameson's words, was 'a prodigious expansion of culture throughout the social realm, to the point at which everything in our social life – from economic value and state power to practices and to the very structure of the psyche itself – can be said to have become "cultural" in some original and as yet untheorised sense'.[13] As politics were spectacularized, commodities aestheticized, consumption eroticized and commerce semioticized, culture seemed to have become the new social 'dominant', as entrenched and pervasive in its own way as religion in the Middle Ages, philosophy in early nineteenth-century Germany or the natural sciences in Victorian Britain. 'Culture' meant that social life was 'constructed', and so mutable, multiple and transient in a way of which both radical activists and consumer experts could approve. But culture was now also a 'second nature' with a vengeance, massively enduring and utterly foundational. Advanced capitalism has pulled off the improbable trick of naturalizing its own forms of life by appealing not to their permanence but to their perishability.

Culture, however, needed yet another component if it was to become thoroughly postmodern. If it put its mark on capitalism, it was equally to put its mark on the left. What had survived of the politically turbulent 1960s was life-style and identity politics, which as the class struggle froze over in the mid-1970s surged increasingly to the fore. The women's movement, hatched in an inhospitably masculinist 1960s but blossoming in the brief gap between the demise of this culture and the onset of global reaction, was joined by other movements for which culture was neither an optional extra nor an idealist distraction, but the very grammar of political struggle. Meanwhile, while the West had been conducting its anxious post-war cultural debates, the colonized world was living through the era of national liberation struggles. Though cultural questions here necessarily took a back seat to political ones, large sectors of the globe were nonetheless being reconstructed by a political current – revolutionary nationalism – whose roots were set deep in the idea of culture.

As these colonial contentions gathered to a head in the Vietnam period, they interbred with the cultural politics of the Western left, in a bizarre yet bracing alliance of Godard and Guevara. But these were also the years of continuing post-imperial migration, when cultural identity in Britain and elsewhere was being pitched into crisis not only by post-imperial anomie, but by the resurgence of the imperial question in the unsettling form of a potentially multicultural nation. Culture was thus also at stake in debates over the very destiny of Western societies, disorientated as they already were by a loss of imperial identity, cultural Americanization, the spreading influence of consumerism and the mass media, and the increasingly articulate voices of ex-working-class intellectuals who had reaped the benefits of higher education without thereby endorsing its ideological values.

What gradually took place was a shift from this politicized culture to cultural politics. Culture in the sense of identity, allegiance, everyday life had severely challenged a philistine, patriarchal, ethnically blinded left. But as national liberation passed into post-coloniality, and the politicized culture of the 1960s and early 1970s gave way to the postmodern 1980s, culture was the supplement which came gradually to oust what it had amplified. As market forces penetrated more deeply into cultural production, while working-class struggles were defeated and socialist forces scattered, culture rose to fame as the 'dominant' both for advanced capitalism and for a range of its opponents. It was a shift highly convenient for some left intellectuals, who could console themselves for the political downturn of their day with the thought that their professional patch had now assumed a fresh, adventurously global significance. A 1970s left politics which had tried to retheorize the place of culture within socialist politics, and had turned eagerly to Gramsci, Freud, Kristeva, Barthes, Fanon, Althusser, Williams, Habermas and others in order to do so, was undermined not by the anti-cultural philistinism of the left itself, as had happened so often before, but by the opposite – by the inflation of its own cultural concerns to the point where they threatened to cut loose from politics altogether.

What threatened those concerns, then, was not starvation but a surfeit. The celebrated 'turn to the subject', with its heady blend of discourse theory, semiotics and psychoanalysis, proved to be a turn away from revolutionary politics, and in some cases from politics as such. If the 1930s left had undersold culture, the postmodern left overvalued it. Indeed it seems the destiny of the concept to be either reified or reduced. As the playwright David Edgar observes, postmodern thought aims

> to pursue the individual ends of the counter-culture while abandoning the more traditional collective means of social democracy, to celebrate the diversity of the new social forces of the 1960s and 1970s at the expense of the challenge they posed to dominant structures, to privilege personal choice over collective action, to validate an individual emotional response to liberal and psychological impoverishment while devaluing the conventional structures of political activity, to break the ideological links between oppositional intellectuals and the poor.[14]

The counter-culture of the 1960s, uncoupled from its political base, modulated into postmodernism. Meanwhile, in the erstwhile colonial world, new states had emerged on the back of a revolutionary nationalism which then either faded from political memory or was vigorously scrubbed from it. It thus became easy to believe that what was at stake there too was less politics than culture, not least as an astonishingly fertile post-colonial writing began to burgeon, and as dissidents who could find no assured identity in a post-political West began to search for it earnestly abroad. Post-colonial societies could also provide a few allegorical points of reference for identity politics in the West. And as the left turned progressively to culture, so in a kind of grotesque mirror-image of it did advanced capitalism, as what used to be called politics, labour, or economics now staged their reappearance as image and information.

This is not, need one say, to equate campaigns against racism with the splendours of digital television. The period which has seen new kinds of dominance has also witnessed new forms of emergence, all the way from peace and ecology movements to human rights agencies and campaigns against poverty and homelessness. In this sense, as we have seen, our culture wars are a four-cornered fight, not a three-cornered one. If there is culture as civility, culture as identity and culture as commercialism, there is also culture as radical protest. As David Edgar puts it:

> First, there is the patrician model, which sees art's role as ennobling, its realm the nation, its organisational form the institution, its repertoire the established canon and works aspiring to join it, its base audience the cultural elite. In traditional opposition to the patrician model is that of the popular: seeing art's primary purpose as entertainment, its realm the market-place, its form the business, its audience mass. In contrast to both is the provocative (both in content and form): defining the role of the arts as challenging, its realm the community, its form the collective, its audience diverse but united in its commitment to change.[15]

Edgar's scheme is suggestive, though it fails to point out that some forms of both patrician and popular culture can be radical in content. It also passes over cultures of identity, whose relation to the politics of change is clearly ambiguous. If identity politics have ranked among the most emancipatory of contemporary movements, some brands of them have also been closed, intolerant and supremacist. Deaf to the need for wider political solidarity, they represent a kind of group individualism which reflects the dominant social ethos as much as it dissents from it. They are common cultures in exactly the sense that Williams does not intend. At the worst, an open society becomes one which encourages a whole range of closed cultures. Liberal pluralism and communitarianism are in this sense mirror-images of one another. The predatory actions of capitalism breed, by way of defensive reaction, a multitude of closed cultures, which the pluralist ideology of capitalism can then celebrate as a rich diversity of life-forms.

Culture became a vital preoccupation of the modern age for a whole range of reasons. There was the emergence for the first time of a commercially organized mass culture, which was felt to pose a calamitous threat to the survival of civilized values. Mass culture was not just an affront to high culture; it sabotaged the whole moral basis of social life. But there was also the role played by culture in cementing the bonds of the nation-state, as well as in providing an increasingly agnostic ruling class with a suitably edifying alternative to religious faith. Cultures in the sense of distinctive ways of life were thrown into dramatic relief by colonialism, confirming the superiority of Western life, but also relativizing the identity of the colonialist powers at just the point where they needed to feel most assured of it. In the post-imperial epoch, this shaking of selfhood was brought nearer home in the form of ethnic immigration, while at the same time changes in the nature of capitalism thrust culture to the forefront through a pervasive aestheticizing of social life. Meanwhile, the drastically shrinking world of transnational capitalism pitched diverse life-forms ever more eclectically together, making men and women at once newly aware of their cultural identities and freshly insecure about them. As class politics appeared to stall in the face of this aggressive new global power-bloc, fresh political currents for which culture in the broad sense was the very stuff of politics flowed in to take their place. At the same time, in the former Soviet bloc, culture became a vital form of political dissent, as the mantle of resistance passed from the politicos to the poets.

In the face of this cultural efflorescence, one sober fact needs to be recalled. The primary problems which we confront in the new millennium – war, famine, poverty, disease, debt, drugs, environmental pollution, the displacement of peoples – are not especially 'cultural' at all. They are not primarily questions of value, symbolism, language, tradition, belonging or identity, least of all the arts. Cultural theorists *qua* cultural theorists have precious little to contribute to their resolution. In the new millennium, astonishingly, humankind faces pretty much the kinds of material problems it always has, with a few novel ones like debt, drugs and nuclear armaments thrown in for good measure. Like any other material issues, these matters are culturally inflected, bound up with beliefs and identities, and increasingly enmeshed in doctrinal systems. But they are cultural problems only in a sense which risks expanding the term to the point of meaninglessness.

Culture is not only what we live by. It is also, in great measure, what we live for. Affection, relationship, memory, kinship, place, community, emotional fulfilment, intellectual enjoyment, a sense of ultimate meaning: these are closer to most of us than charters of human rights or trade treaties. Yet culture can also be too close for comfort. This very intimacy is likely to grow morbid and obsessional unless it is set in an enlightened political context, one which can temper these immediacies with more abstract, but also in a way more generous, affiliations. We have seen how culture has assumed a new political importance. But it has grown at the same time immodest and overweening. It is time, while acknowledging its significance, to put it back in its place.

Notes

1 Versions of Culture

1 David Harvey, *Justice, Nature and the Geography of Difference* (Oxford, 1996), pp. 186–8.
2 A valuable account of this lineage is to be found in David Lloyd and Paul Thomas, *Culture and the State* (New York and London, 1998). See also Ian Hunter, *Culture and Government* (London, 1988), esp. ch. 3.
3 S.T. Coleridge, *On the Constitution of Church and State* (1830, reprinted Princeton, 1976), pp. 42–3.
4 Friedrich Schiller, *On the Aesthetic Education of Man, In a Series of Letters* (Oxford, 1967), p. 17.
5 See Raymond Williams, *Keywords* (London, 1976), pp. 76–82. It is interesting to note that Williams had completed much of the work on his entry on culture in this volume as early as the essay of 1953 referred to in note 7 below.
6 See Norbert Elias, *The Civilising Process* (1939, reprinted Oxford, 1994), ch. 1.
7 Raymond Williams, 'The Idea of Culture', in John McIlroy and Sallie Westwood (eds), *Border Country: Raymond Williams in Adult Education* (Leicester, 1993), p. 60.
8 See Robert J.C. Young, *Colonial Desire* (London and New York, 1995), ch. 2. This is the best brief introduction available to the modern idea of culture, and its dubious racist overtones. As far as Enlightenment cultural relativism goes, Swift's *Gulliver's Travels* is an exemplary case in point.
9 See ibid., p. 79.

10 Johann Gottfried von Herder, *Reflections on the Philosophy of the History of Mankind* (1784–91, reprinted Chicago, 1968), p. 49.
11 See for example John Fiske, *Understanding Popular Culture* (London, 1989) and *Reading the Popular* (London, 1989). For a critical commentary on this case, see Jim McGuigan, *Cultural Populism* (London, 1992).
12 For a lucid treatment of topics in cultural anthropology, see John Beattie, *Other Cultures* (London, 1964).
13 Young, *Colonial Desire*, p. 53.
14 Franz Boas, *Race, Language and Culture* (1940, reprinted Chicago and London, 1982), p. 30.
15 Edward Said, *Culture and Imperialism* (London, 1993), p. xxix.
16 Schiller, *On the Aesthetic Education of Man*, p. 141.
17 Ibid., p. 146.
18 Ibid., p. 151.
19 Williams, *Keywords*, p. 81.
20 For a critique of such Romantic nationalism, see Terry Eagleton, 'Nationalism and the Case of Ireland', *New Left Review* no. 234 (March/April, 1999).
21 See, for this case, Ernest Gellner, *Thought and Change* (London, 1964) and *Nations and Nationalism* (Oxford, 1983).
22 Geoffrey Hartman, *The Fateful Question of Culture* (New York, 1997), p. 211.
23 The phrase alludes to Raymond Williams's celebrated formulation 'Masses are other people', in *Culture and Society 1780–1950* (London, 1958, reprinted Harmondsworth, 1963), p. 289.
24 Fredric Jameson, 'On "Cultural Studies"', *Social Text* no. 34 (1993), p. 34.
25 Jairus Banaji, 'The Crisis of British Anthropology', *New Left Review* no. 64 (November/December, 1970).
26 Quoted ibid., p. 79 n.
27 See Claude Lévi-Strauss, *Anthropologie structurale* (Paris, 1958) and *La Pensée sauvage* (Paris, 1966).
28 Marshall Sahlins, *Culture and Practical Reason* (Chicago and London, 1976), p. 6.
29 Andrew Milner, *Cultural Materialism* (Melbourne, 1993), pp. 3 and 5.
30 Williams, *Culture and Society*, p. 17.

2 Culture in Crisis

1 Margaret S. Archer, *Culture and Agency* (Cambridge, 1996), p. 1.
2 Edward Sapir, *The Psychology of Culture* (New York, 1994), p. 84. For a diverse set of definitions of culture, see A.L. Kroeber and C. Kluckhohn, 'Culture: A Critical Review of Concepts and Definitions', *Papers of the Peabody Museum of American Archaeology and Ethnology*, vol. 47 (Harvard, 1952).
3 Raymond Williams, *Culture and Society 1780–1950* (London, 1958, reprinted Harmondsworth, 1963), p. 307.
4 Andrew Milner, *Cultural Materialism* (Melbourne, 1993), p. 1
5 Clifford Geertz, *The Interpretation of Cultures* (London, 1975), p. 5.
6 Raymond Williams, *Culture* (Glasgow, 1981), p.13.
7 E.B. Tylor, *Primitive Culture* (London, 1871), vol. 1, p. 1.
8 Zygmunt Bauman, 'Legislators and Interpreters: Culture as Ideology of Intellectuals', in Hans Haferkamp (ed.), *Social Structure and Culture* (New York, 1989), p. 315.
9 Stuart Hall, 'Culture and the State', in Open University, *The State and Popular Culture* (Milton Keynes, 1982), p. 7. A valuable summary of arguments over culture is to be found in R. Billington, S. Strawbridge, L. Greensides and A. Fitzsimons, *Culture and Society: A Sociology of Culture* (London, 1991).
10 John Frow, *Cultural Studies and Cultural Value* (Oxford, 1995), p. 3.
11 Raymond Williams, 'The Idea of Culture', in John McIlroy and Sallie Westwood (eds), *Border Country: Raymond Williams in Adult Education* (Leicester, 1993), p. 61.
12 Williams, *Culture and Society*, p. 16.
13 Raymond Williams, *The Long Revolution* (London, 1961, reprinted Harmondsworth, 1965), p. 42.
14 Ibid., pp. 64 and 63. If I may add a personal note here, Williams discovered the notion of ecology long before it became fashionable, and once described it to me, who had never heard of it previously, as 'the study of the interrelation of elements in a living system'. This is interestingly close to his definition of culture here.
15 Geoffrey Hartman, *The Fateful Question of Culture* (New York, 1997), p. 30.
16 Julien Benda, *The Treason of the Intellectuals* (Paris, 1927), p. 29.
17 Edward Said, *Culture and Imperialism* (London, 1993), p. xiv.

18 Francis Mulhern, 'The Politics of Cultural Studies', in Ellen Meiksins Wood and John Bellamy Foster (eds), *In Defense of History* (New York, 1997), p. 50.
19 Richard Rorty, 'Human Rights, Rationality, and Sentimentality', in Obrad Savic (ed.), *The Politics of Human Rights* (London, 1999), p. 80.

3 Culture Wars

1 Fredric Jameson, 'Marx's Purloined Letter', in Michael Sprinker (ed.), *Ghostly Demarcations* (London, 1999), p. 51.
2 For an effective dismantling of the high culture/low culture antithesis, see John Frow, *Cultural Studies and Cultural Value* (Oxford, 1995), pp. 23–6.
3 See in particular Richard Rorty, *Irony, Contingency, and Solidarity* (Cambridge, 1989).
4 Kate Soper, *What Is Nature?* (Oxford, 1995), p. 65.
5 Ruth Benedict, *Patterns of Culture* (1935, reprinted London, 1961), p. 4.
6 For some useful comments on this hyphenation, see Tzvetan Todorov, *Human Diversity* (Cambridge, Mass., 1993), ch. 3.
7 Jean-François Lyotard, *The Postmodern Condition* (Manchester, 1984), p. 76.
8 Aijaz Ahmad, 'Reconciling Derrida: Specters of Marx and Deconstructive Politics', in Sprinker (ed.), *Ghostly Demarcations*, p. 100.
9 Richard Kearney, *Visions of Europe* (Dublin, 1992), p. 83.
10 Ibid., p. 43.
11 Robert Young points out that Hebraism for Arnold is a kind of philistinism, which implies – since 'philistine' originally means 'non-Jew' – that the Jews are non-Jewish. Cultivated Englishmen then take over the role of the chosen people. See *Colonial Desire,* p. 58.
12 Meera Nanda, 'Against Social De(con)struction of Science: Cautionary Tales from the Third World', in Ellen Meiksins Wood and John Bellamy Foster (eds), *In Defense of History* (New York, 1997), p. 75.
13 Raymond Williams, *Towards 2000* (London, 1983), p. 198.
14 Francis Mulhern, 'Towards 2000, Or News from You-Know-Where', in Terry Eagleton (ed.), *Raymond Williams: Critical Perspectives* (Oxford, 1989), p. 86.

15 See Paul James, *Nation Formation* (London, 1996), ch. 1.
16 See Frank Farrell, *Subjectivity, Realism and Postmodernism* (Cambridge, 1996).

4 Culture and Nature

1 Kate Soper, *What Is Nature?* (Oxford, 1995), pp. 132–3.
2 Richard Rorty, 'Human Rights, Rationality, and Sentimentality', in Obrad Savic (ed.), *The Politics of Human Rights* (London, 1999), p. 72. Rorty seems to assume in this essay that the only basis for the notion of a universal human nature is the idea of rationality, which is far from the case.
3 Sebastiano Timpanaro, *On Materialism* (London, 1975), p. 45.
4 See Soper, *What Is Nature?*, ch. 4.
5 Slavoj Žižek, *The Abyss of Freedom/Ages of the World* (Ann Arbor, 1997), pp. 50 and 51.
6 Edward Bond, *Lear* (London, 1972), p. viii.
7 Friedrich Nietzsche, *Beyond Good and Evil*, in Walter Kaufmann (ed.), *Basic Writings of Nietzsche* (New York, 1968), p. 307.
8 Friedrich Nietzsche, *On the Genealogy of Morals*, ibid., pp. 550 and 498.
9 William Empson, *Some Versions of Pastoral* (London, 1966), p. 114.
10 Timpanaro, *On Materialism*, p. 50.

5 Towards a Common Culture

1 I have drawn in what follows on my essay 'Eliot and a Common Culture', in Graham Martin (ed.), *Eliot in Perspective* (London, 1970).
2 T.S. Eliot, *Notes Towards the Definition of Culture* (London, 1948), p. 120. Further references to this work will be given in parentheses after quotations. The title of the work is an interesting blend of modesty and authoritativeness: 'notes', but towards 'the definition'.
3 Raymond Williams, *Culture and Society 1780–1950* (London, 1958), p. 234.
4 T.S. Eliot, *The Idea of a Christian Society* (London, 1939), pp. 28–9.
5 Louis Althusser, *Lenin and Philosophy* (London, 1971), p. 167.

6 See Pierre Bourdieu, *Outline of a Theory of Practice* (Cambridge, 1977).
7 Eliot, *The Idea of a Christian Society*, p. 30.
8 Williams, *Culture and Society*, p. 334.
9 Ibid., p. 335.
10 Ibid., p. 238.
11 For accounts of these contentions, see Will Kymlicka, *Liberalism, Community, and Culture* (Oxford, 1989), and Stephen Mulhall and Adam Swift, *Liberals and Communitarians* (Oxford, 1992).
12 Raymond Williams, *Marxism and Literature* (Oxford, 1977), p. 122.
13 Fredric Jameson, 'Postmodernism, Or the Cultural Logic of Late Capitalism', *New Left Review* no. 146 (July, 1984), p. 87.
14 David Edgar (ed.), *State of Play* (London, 1999), p. 25.
15 Ibid., p. 11.

Index

Index

Index